PRAISE FOR *The Just Church*

The American church doesn't prin...
cution but from inaction. Jim Ma...
Christians to practice Christianity...
from apathy to action.

Richard Stearns
President of World Vision US and author of *The Hole in Our Gospel*

Jim Martin understands that following Jesus requires us to move past mere good intentions and into the rewarding adventure of seeking justice and rescue for our neighbors in desperate need. *The Just Church* not only provides a convincing call to action, but it offers church communities the desperately needed handles to take next steps with clarity and conviction. This is a must-have resource for any who have concern for the oppressed but have felt powerless to act.

Mark Batterson
Lead pastor and *New York Times* bestselling author

Justice is about discipleship, and what the world needs most is healthy people following Jesus. Jim Martin loves the local church, and *The Just Church* is all about equipping and empowering the church to follow where Jesus leads!

Christine Caine
Founder of The A21 Campaign

If there is an organization with the authority to speak on the church's pursuit of justice, it is International Justice Mission. If there is a leader with the authority to speak as one who has been there, who has tested it in the local church and seen amazing advances, it is Jim Martin. I wholeheartedly recommend this book!

Ram Gidoomal
Board chair, The Lausanne Movement

Jim Martin's profound book suggests that justice is not only about mission, but also about our own discipleship. Along the way there are many stories of both success and failure, all of which become valuable teaching points. The work of IJM around the world is brilliantly inspiring, and so is this book. *The Just Church* captures the heartbeat of a commitment to Christ and to his justice movement.

Matt Redman
Worship leader and songwriter

This is the book I have been waiting for—a thoughtful and thought-provoking look at how discipleship and justice work are inextricably connected. If your heart has been broken by the news of slavery and abuse around the world, and if you have ever wondered how you can generate or participate in a sustained response to injustice, read this book! Nothing has stretched and grown my faith like my attempts to take God's heart for justice seriously. This book is an incredibly inspiring resource for doing just that.

Sara Groves
Singer/songwriter

There is so much injustice in our world today, and organizations like International Justice Mission do a huge amount to fight it, particularly through the work they do to free children, women, and men from slavery; bring the perpetrators to justice; set the captives free; and care for them. I welcome this book as it seeks to help churches get more involved in this issue which is so close to God's heart.

Nicky Gumbel
Vicar, Holy Trinity, Brompton, UK, and developer of the Alpha Course

Compassionate, realistic, down-to-earth, and very easy to read, *The Just Church* speaks powerfully into an issue that is a key part of the church's integral biblical mission and a stark test of the church's authenticity and integrity.

Christopher J. H. Wright
International director, Langham Partnership, and author of *The Mission of God* and *The Mission of God's People*

The Just Church is as practical as it is transformative. It's about how discipleship and "doing justice" are linked, and can literally change a congregation from the inside out. I can't wait to get this book into the hands of the small groups in our church—and to the future pastors in our seminary.

Dr. Stephen Hayner
President, Columbia Theological Seminary

THE JUST CHURCH

Becoming a risk-taking, justice-seeking,
disciple-making congregation

Jim Martin

A resource of The IJM
Institute for Biblical Justice
Learn more at IJM.org

INTERNATIONAL
JUSTICE MISSION®

TYNDALE™
MOMENTUM

An Imprint of
Tyndale House Publishers, Inc.

Visit Tyndale online at www.tyndale.com.

Visit Tyndale Momentum online at www.tyndalemomentum.com.

TYNDALE is a registered trademark of Tyndale House Publishers, Inc. *Tyndale Momentum* and the Tyndale Momentum logo are trademarks of Tyndale House Publishers, Inc. Tyndale Momentum is an imprint of Tyndale House Publishers, Inc.

The Just Church: Becoming a Risk-Taking, Justice-Seeking, Disciple-Making Congregation

Designed by Stephen Vosloo

Edited by Jonathan Schindler

Library of Congress Cataloging-in-Publication Data

Martin, Jim.
   The just church : becoming a risk-taking, justice-seeking, disciple-making congregation / by Jim Martin.
      p. cm.
   Includes bibliographical references (p.   ) and index.
   ISBN 978-1-4143-7128-3 (sc)
1. Christianity and justice. 2. Church. I. Title.
   BR115.J8M385 2012
   261.8—dc23   2012019457

Printed in the United States of America

18   17   16   15   14   13   12
 7   6   5   4   3   2   1

To my friends and fellow pilgrims
at The River Church Community

Contents

Foreword

IT'S AWKWARD when you extend an invitation to friends and all you get is a pile of polite regrets. It's even worse when you realize that they declined not because they weren't interested in coming, but because you invited them so badly. And honestly, that's the way I feel when I recall my earliest attempts to invite fellow Christians into the biblical work of seeking justice in the world—and why I am so thrilled about this new book by my colleague Jim Martin.

In 1994 I had returned to the United States after leading the UN investigation of the Rwandan genocide and was working closely with a small group to launch the fledgling ministry that would become International Justice Mission. We were eager for our little team to be used by God to bring rescue and hope to people suffering violent abuse and oppression. But we were just as eager to invite fellow Christians to join us in God's powerful and passionate work of justice in the world—and to provide local churches with a practical vehicle for partnership in the work. We were excited to have our fellow believers join us in what we were discovering to be a struggle of divine calling, great difficulty, and deep joy. We longed for co-laborers in the prayers, the rescue, and the restoration. We sought partnership and companionship in the transformation by God's grace of our own lives, as well as of those we sought to serve.

But we knew this would be an unfamiliar invitation. In most of the churches we connected with in the mid-1990s, justice was at best seen as an extra-credit option to the "legitimate" work of the church—a sort of semi-respectable hobby or extracurricular activity for people who happened to be interested in that sort of thing. At worst, justice was seen as a threatening distraction from the parts of God's call that "really" mattered. But in most cases, it was simply not *seen* at all.

But fresh winds were blowing through the church, and new openings were presented to extend this invitation. In fact, I vividly remember the first time I got to stand before a congregation and try out my new rally cry to justice ministry. Granted, it was an evening service, in August, in a church where the pastor owed one of my relatives a favor—but there I was with a full opportunity to share God's passion for justice from the Scriptures, to describe the urgent need in the world, and to extend Christ's exciting invitation to be his instruments of rescue and restoration in the most desperate places.

And . . . I bombed.

You could see it on everyone's faces as the service concluded and they rushed for the exits gasping for fresh air. I had drained all the oxygen out of the sanctuary with my depressing stories of horrible injustice and my soul-crushing, guilt-inducing tour through Scripture, proof-texting God's outrage about all this ugly oppression and abuse. As the last few ashen-faced believers trailed out of the church, I looked to my relatives, hoping to receive whatever implausible encouragement they might offer—but even they couldn't fake it. It was as if I had been in charge of inviting friends to a birthday party and had managed to make it sound like a seminar on aging.

Amidst all the accurate data about slavery, sex trafficking, torture, and abuse, and all the biblical teaching on God's beating heart for justice, I had left out the one truth that was larger than all of it: *hope*! Rather than inspire and empower these earnest Christ-followers to respond to God's holy calling, I'd left them in the paralysis of despair. I hadn't shared the joy and contentment of knowing that the struggle against injustice is *God's* struggle—and that we are simply called to do our little part and experience him as he equips his church to do the work. I hadn't shared the power of the invitation: God's call isn't to *feel bad about injustice*—but to *do justice*! Marvelously, God never gives us a mission without granting us the power to do it. And through the mission, he also promises to change us—to make us more like his Son.

Thankfully, this is the message of hope that now fills these pages—and today, the church is more than ready to receive it.

By his grace, over the past fifteen years God has ignited a movement of transformation in his church—a movement of passion and action on behalf of millions who are victims of injustice in our world. Today the church is awake and alive to God's call to justice, and we are praising him for this clear evidence of his Spirit and the many miracles of restoration and rescue he has done through and in the church.

And we sense he is just getting started.

So now—instead of the scramble for the exits prompted by my first rendering of the invitation—we have a very different and very good challenge. Today, more and more of God's people have joyfully accepted the invitation to justice ministry, and they are now looking for their place in the movement and for tangible ways to join Christ in the work. The challenge now is to provide these believers with a clear, Christ-centered pathway to concretely "seek justice, rescue the oppressed, defend the orphan, plead for the widow" (Isaiah 1:17).

This book is our answer to that challenge. It will equip you and your church to engage in God's struggle for justice in this world.

But at its heart, this is not just a book about joining the justice movement or about helping International Justice Mission—*it's about the way God transforms his church and molds us all into the likeness of his Son.* It's about discipleship. It's about the utterly unique way that God uses the struggle for justice to draw us closer to himself—through desperate dependence upon him and through extraordinary experiences of his power. Over and over again, we have seen churches find spiritual renewal and a depth of maturity in Christ like they have never experienced before through the transforming crucible of justice ministry.

My IJM colleagues and I have learned a lot over these last fifteen years of companionship with the body of Christ in the struggle for justice, and we are eager to share what God has been teaching us. The book you hold in your hands is an intensely practical guidebook to this uniquely fruitful path for spiritual growth. And in my view, you could not have a better guide than my friend Jim Martin.

Jim wants to see churches flourish in the work of justice because he loves justice; but more than that, Jim wants to see churches flourish in the work of justice because *Jim loves the church*. He takes genuine delight in the way God has chosen the church as the instrument through which he wants to carry out his redeeming work in the world—and his delight is contagious.

As a pastor, he *gets* the church—with all its beauty, strength, divine power, brokenness, flaws, and foibles. His voice is one of pastoral encouragement, because he has been there. Jim knows that God wants to ignite the church to light up the world with his justice—not because of the perfection of the church, but simply out of God's grace and eagerness to invite every person into his redemptive work and missional purpose in the world. And what Jim most fundamentally knows is that everything in the church is *about God and our relationship with God*. For Jim, pursuing justice is about pursuing the God of justice, never some isolated external goal or accomplishment. His goal is to prepare your church for the work of justice—not through slick programming or human effort, but through a deep knowledge of God's good love, a real communion with our Father who loves justice.

And this is a powerful thing—for each of us and for a world waiting in need.

If I could go back to the brothers and sisters I left sitting paralyzed in despair on that first Sunday evening service, *this* is the book I'd want to bring with me to share. I'd want to let them know that violent injustice is *real*; but more deeply and more wonderfully, I'd want them to know how eager our God is to equip them to do the work of justice and in the process to make us more like his Son.

Whether you're taking your first step in this journey or seeking fuel after many years in the trenches of justice ministry, I'm so glad you've decided to read this book. By doing so, you are following Jesus into the deep waters of discipleship, where his power is made perfect in our weakness, where he brings his love to those in most desperate need, and where "your light shall rise in the darkness and your gloom be like the noonday" (Isaiah 58:10).

Gary Haugen
President and CEO of International Justice Mission

Introduction

IT SEEMED like a strange place for a pastor to be sitting. But there I sat, slightly wide-eyed, advancing slide after slide of images. In the room with me were more than sixty of the most significant officials in the region's public justice system: judges, prosecutors, social workers, medical doctors, and police. We'd all sat in rapt attention as the lab-coated medical professional walked us through the history of sexual abuse definitions dating all the way back to the Code of Hammurabi and arriving at the definition according to current legal code. She had now arrived at the more technical part of her presentation, during which she carefully explained the proper forensic medical examination procedure to discover, document, and collect physical evidence of sexual abuse. On her cue, I advanced through more than a hundred slides containing photographs at 10x magnification of actual exams with actual victims. The presenter pointed out in careful detail the telltale signs left behind by sexual abuse.

And as I sat, watching the difficult and graphic images play across the screen, I couldn't help but reflect on what was happening. Representatives from my church, The River Church Community in San Jose, California, had formed a partnership with a Peruvian organization called Paz y Esperanza—a group of Christian lawyers, investigators, and psychologists working to combat an epidemic of sexual violence perpetrated against children in their region of Peru. We had initially entered the partnership looking for some small way to serve this courageous organization. But before long we were almost completely overwhelmed, not just by the scope of the problem, but by the vision these Peruvian brothers and sisters had for how the church could and should respond.

From the beginning of the relationship, we had been running just to keep up. But fast-forward a mere two years from our initial meeting with Paz y Esperanza, and there we sat in a room with the leaders of Huánuco, Peru's public justice system. The professional and knowledgeable presenter in the lab coat was Julie, a nurse-practitioner from our church. Also on our small team from The River were two mental-health professionals whose work focused on children at risk and whose clinical experience included dealing with sexual-abuse trauma. I was on the team as well, but since my skills and expertise were more pastoral, about all I was equipped to do at this particular meeting was run the slides.

What I found most remarkable during the meeting was the way we could almost feel the officials' commitment growing as we spoke. Key officials in the public justice system were adapting their definitions of what constitutes sexual abuse to align with internationally recognized standards. They were adopting the latest practices. The woefully out-of-date physical exam protocol was being replaced by an updated set of techniques that would gather the necessary evidence to offer survivors of sexual abuse the protections Peruvian law afforded them. Not only was the sexual abuse of children being discussed in public, but the officials attending the consultation were committing to real, practical, and effective change. Things were changing, and we weren't there just to watch them happen; we got to participate in the miracles. The battle, of course, continues to this day—as does the partnership between

The River and Paz y Esperanza. But this meeting, held on an otherwise normal Tuesday, represented a turning point.

The extent of the impact we witnessed in just five years astounded me. But equally shocking was the shift we witnessed over the next ten years in churches like The River. What we saw was that issues of injustice—such as the unprosecuted sexual abuse of children—were appearing on the radar screens of more and more churches. The church at large seemed to have moved from almost complete silence on the subject of justice to a remarkable verbosity—to the point where lately church and ministry literature and websites are seasoned with words like *justice, poverty, hunger, trafficking, slavery,* and *abolition.*

While it may be hard to pinpoint how these difficult issues have found their way into the church's sphere of attention, we should celebrate the arrival of the church to meet these important challenges. We may protest that the church (particularly the Protestant evangelical church) has shown up late, that other branches of the historical church have been there all along; we may express concern that the church is sometimes clumsy when it engages. But let us celebrate that a discernible movement of God's Spirit is afoot, capturing the attention of churches of all shapes and sizes, bending the imagination and energy of God's people back toward justice.

Last century, at the close of World War II, this same group of churches was struggling to come to grips with issues such as hunger, poverty, and homelessness. The 1940s and 1950s saw a dramatic increase in the number of Christian humanitarian organizations.[1] Many of these were formed by faithful followers of Jesus who in their World War II service had seen a kind of poverty and suffering previously unknown to them. The creation of these organizations was their faithful and courageous response to the needs they saw and an expression of their willingness to explore what the gospel of Jesus might have to say about such suffering. After more than fifty years of God's patient work with his church, in my experience, it is difficult to find an evangelical church in the United States that does *not* have some sort of mercy program to address the issues of neighbors suffering for lack of basic needs.

Savvy readers will no doubt note that branches of the historical church have been involved in issues of justice for decades, centuries, even millennia. And they will also know that inner-city congregations of all types have long sounded the call for the church to engage injustice. These churches have articulated specific needs ranging from reforming public schools underserving the neediest students, to challenging unfair wages, to ending racial discrimination, to relieving hunger. Certainly these courageous pastors and churches are leaders to whom we are all indebted. This book and the movement it describes would not exist without them.

But for the purposes of this book, I will define the issue of justice more narrowly. The justice issues of concern in these pages are those involving the violent oppression of the most vulnerable in our world—most often in the Two-Thirds World.[2] I do not intend to imply that this need is greater than or should compete with or supplant local issues of justice more broadly defined. What I seek to call attention to is the remarkable (and welcome) shift currently taking place that has brought the suffering of victims of violence in the Two-Thirds World into sharp focus among resourced, comfortable evangelical churches elsewhere.

I have spent the last decade of ministry involved in the church's response to issues of violent oppression—first as a pastor of a North American church deeply involved in the fight against the unprosecuted sexual abuse of minors in a small community in Peru, and more recently as the vice president of church mobilization with International Justice Mission (IJM), a human rights organization whose staff are motivated by the Bible's call to seek justice. From this unique vantage point, I can faithfully report that the growing justice movement is exciting and real. Though new and sometimes flawed, the church's engagement is as creative as it is courageous. Faithful followers of Jesus are taking significant risks to invest their time, talents, and resources in God's work of rescuing the oppressed, defending the orphan, and pleading for the widow (see Isaiah 1:17).

Shallow Motivations

Because the suffering endured by victims of injustice in our world can be overwhelming to contemplate, affluent evangelicals the world over have often chosen (whether consciously or not) to isolate themselves from such horrors and insulate themselves from the charged emotions injustice-related suffering elicits. However, almost any exposure to the statistics—and particularly the stories of the many victims of violent oppression around the world—produces significant unrest for people of reasonably good heart. This turbulence of soul often leads to a burst of activity—a desperate search for some meaningful way to engage in the issues.

Add to this exposure the growing awareness in many churches that the Scriptures speak with remarkable clarity and regularity about the issue of injustice. Indeed, a simple reading of the Old Testament alone reveals this. With the understandable exception of idolatry, the Old Testament addresses injustice with greater frequency than any other issue.[3] There is a growing awareness that God has always been deeply concerned for those on the margins of society, those whose lack of power and voice make them extraordinarily vulnerable. Further, people of faith are seeing once again that from God's perspective, God's people have always been his solution to the suffering of the world's vulnerable.

Both the compelling nature of the need and the reality of God's call to engage are often reasons enough for action. I have been in

xx || THE JUST CHURCH

contact with hundreds of churches where newfound passion has propelled them several steps down the road to direct engagement in the battle against injustice. But the issues of violent oppression are by nature so very dark, complex, confusing, chaotic, and taboo that good intentions, passion, and even outrage often fuel involvement for a surprisingly short time. The inevitable loss of traction and feelings of disappointment and helplessness can and often do thwart the plans of the well-intentioned. As churches engage issues of oppression, they often find that the faith they bring is not rugged enough to survive the desperation they inevitably feel as they get close to the violence of injustice. The need to stay "in control," the need to be "safe," and the need for "success" deflate the passion and hope they felt so clearly at the outset. This often results in waning commitment or in a commitment to remain only on the surface of the issue.

There has already been much written on the shape and nature of the problem of injustice as it exists in today's world. In these pages I will not add to the body of statistics that have been carefully gathered and disseminated by others.[4] My primary interest is to tell the story of how and why the church is engaging in the fight against injustice. The *how* of the story is inspiring and compelling, and it is my hope that it will propel many more churches to engage while offering helpful, concrete models for that engagement. The *why* of the church's engagement may be surprising. While the statistics, the need, and the call of God are often the primary impetus for my friends around the world who are taking risks to engage, there is another benefit that few of us expected when we began this journey. What we've found is that the work of justice is some of the most fertile ground for discipleship that we've ever experienced. The places of violent oppression and abuse that may seem utterly God-forsaken are in fact the places where we have most deeply experienced the presence and power of God.

The call to the work of justice is therefore not God sending his church *out* to a place where God cannot be found. Rather, God is inviting us *into* the place where he is already at work. It is here, among the world's most vulnerable, that the Good News of God turns out to be very good indeed. In the work of justice, our good God is offering us what we so deeply desire in our churches. In the work of justice, God is beckoning us to experience his profound love for us and for the vulnerable of this world. The call to fight against injustice is therefore the call to intimacy with God and to deep discipleship.

That this is true should not be surprising. In the Scriptures, there is a repeated theme of faithful people seeking just such a palpable sense of God's presence. The Old Testament tells the repeated story of the Israelites desperately seeking intimacy with God only to become frustrated that he seems elusive. They continually engage in and refine their forms of worship by offering more and more lambs and goats and bulls. They engage in solemn assemblies and appointed festivals in an effort to seek God, but to their frustration, he is not found.

I perceive some of this struggle in my own church and in many of the churches my friends lead and attend. We continually tweak the mode of our worship in an effort to connect more deeply with God. Surely a new song, an ancient hymn, a new form of worship, or an old rite will give us that sense of connection we crave. Surely more liturgy, less liturgy, a better band, no band, or better preaching will win back for us that sense of God's presence in our midst. I think our willingness to examine our forms of worship is well-intentioned and often good, but it can produce a tendency to become entirely focused on these things to the exclusion of the clear commands of our Father. When left to fester, this disconnect becomes a sinful pattern that the Scriptures describe again and again.

This, in fact, is the context of the opening to the book of Isaiah:

> What to me is the multitude of your sacrifices?
>> says the LORD;
> I have had enough of burnt offerings of rams
>> and the fat of fed beasts;
> I do not delight in the blood of bulls,
>> or of lambs, or of goats. . . .
>
> Bringing offerings is futile;
>> incense is an abomination to me.
> New moon and sabbath and calling of convocation—
>> I cannot endure solemn assemblies with iniquity.
> Your new moons and your appointed festivals
>> my soul hates;
> they have become a burden to me,
>> I am weary of bearing them.
> When you stretch out your hands,
>> I will hide my eyes from you;
> even though you make many prayers,
>> I will not listen;
>> your hands are full of blood. . . .
>> Learn to do good;
> seek justice,
>> rescue the oppressed,
> defend the orphan,
>> plead for the widow.
>
> ISAIAH 1:11, 13-15, 17

The Israelites' pietistic pursuit of God had become so disconnected—particularly from the needy and vulnerable around them—that God called it *sin*. He goes so far as to say they have blood on their hands. The wonderful promise, however, is that for the church that is willing to learn to do good and seek justice, God is very willing to be found.

That's what this book is about. If there is a surprise contained in these chapters, it is this: Through the pursuit of justice we find our way to deep intimacy with a God who loves us and calls us into his work not only for the good of others, but for our own good as well. The work of justice, therefore, is as much about *discipleship* as it is about *mission*. You'll find this book divided into two roughly equal parts. Part 1 deals with the interrelatedness of discipleship and justice. In it we'll walk through the role that risk and even failure play in the strengthening of our faith. We'll talk about how the church of Jesus is hardwired for life-and-death struggle in our world and why opting in to that struggle is a great way to find the abundant life Jesus promises—a life full of belief, trust, joy, and deep discipleship. Part 2 lays out a practical approach to what it looks like to become a "just church." In it you'll find a practical three-step process many churches have followed on their journey into justice ministry. You'll also find the stories of some of these churches themselves, along with a huge number of resources to get you on your way.

Two Prerequisites

In my work with church members and church leaders over the last several years, I have found that one question is often on their minds as they begin to engage injustice. Leaders especially have wanted to know: As churches attempt to engage in the work of justice, what are the main reasons they fail?

It's an interesting and understandable question. Violent injustice is an environment far more complex and chaotic than most churches are accustomed to. Success can be hard to define, and failure often seems inevitable. As with anything hard, it will require the very best of our hearts, souls, and minds. For us to engage in a healthy and sustainable way, it will require all of the common spiritual disciplines, including prayer, worship, stillness, study, and so on. But my answer to this specific question has been direct and simple. In my experience, there are two reasons that leaders, churches, and individuals either lose heart or fail to find meaningful engagement. The first is a lack of courage; the second is a lack of humility.

Courage is an essential virtue for any missional church. And as churches seek to step into the work of biblical justice, the need for courage becomes paramount. Mobilizing resources, people, and expertise to engage violent forces of injustice will require us to learn things we do not yet know, explore areas that are unfamiliar to us, and encounter a kind of darkness we would much rather ignore. Stepping through the unknown and into darkness requires a significant amount of courage. And a strange thing tends to happen to churches, leaders, and disciples as we get older. We become less and less comfortable with risk. In fact, early successes can ruin us for future risks. Early mold-breaking and courageous innovation all too often become memorialized as program and procedure. We end up preferring the known, the safe bet, the easy and clear ministry option.

If we are to engage violent injustice, courage will be required of us. Courage to learn what needs to be learned, to explore new frontiers of ministry, and especially to engage where we hear the Spirit of God calling us to engage, even—and perhaps supremely—when we feel that what we are being asked to do is not within our power. Churches that lack courage lack the necessary equipment to pursue justice.

Churches that lack humility, on the other hand, can become dangerous in the pursuit of justice. Experts in the field will be among the first to say that a learning posture is essential to success—that a research-based, bridge-building approach to the complexity of engaging violent injustice is an absolute necessity. But learning and supporting are not postures the proud can easily take. All too often the church has shown up courageously but without humility. The results are almost always disastrous: broken relationships, ineffectiveness, frustration, wasted resources, and in many cases, harm done to those the church intended to help. Humility is essential to the kind of partnership that the work of justice requires: humility to listen to the voices of experts in the field, humility to listen especially when those voices of expertise issue from the church in the Two-Thirds World—humility to follow rather than lead.

For the church to be the church, we must embody both values simultaneously. When we lack courage, we almost inevitably settle for a deflated, anemic version of church. When we lack humility, we become incapable of partnership, unable to hear the voices of those we seek to serve, and we run the risk of dangerous overreach. But the good news, in my experience, is that it is hard to overestimate the power unleashed when both virtues are found in the same body. Regardless of size, tradition, or geography, the most successful churches are marked by both courage *and* humility. And they are finding that God's call to engage violent injustice is a call to be the humble and courageous church—the just church. Nothing more and nothing less.

Snap here with your smartphone or visit the link for a video introduction with Jim Martin as he invites you to join the mission of *The Just Church.*

www.tyndal.es/JustChurchIntro

PART 1

Justice, Discipleship, and the Failure Point of Faith

CHAPTER 1

The Failure Point

ONE OF THE BEST things about my job is getting to work with people like Blair. For more than three years, Blair directed the work of IJM in one of our South Asia offices. Much of what IJM knows about freeing slaves from the rice mills, brick kilns, farms, and rock quarries that become the scenes of their violent and prolonged captivity comes from the hard-won, operation-by-operation learning curve that Blair and his team laboriously climbed during his years in the field. By freeing hundreds of slaves through the patient, professional, and steady application of hard work, Blair now occupies some of the most rarefied air of the human rights community, along with legendary figures such as William Wilberforce and Harriet Tubman—though in his humility, he will almost certainly be embarrassed when he reads this comparison.

Blair is now based out of Washington, DC, where he serves as the regional director for all of IJM's offices in South Asia. I take advantage of having lunch with him about every chance I get. I enjoy these conversations for several reasons, not the least of which is that Blair is one of the funniest people I know. His considerable intelligence and quick wit make him a lot of fun to share a meal with. But more than that, as a pastor, I find myself both mystified and fascinated by one question in particular: Where do people like Blair come from?

There is little mystery as to what produces a well-qualified and very capable lawyer, and Blair, a graduate of Wake Forest with a professional background in corporate law, is a classic example of the breed. But among lawyers, even good lawyers, the ability to manage and lead teams of people is a surprisingly rare gift. Blair has this gift. Beyond this, more perplexing to me are the questions that have to do with faith development and discipleship for someone like Blair. What produces people like Blair, who consistently make the kinds of Kingdom-oriented choices he has made and continue to take the kinds of risks he has taken? Certainly he could be working for some high-powered law firm. Both the prestige and the financial rewards would make possible for him a kind of life that is likely out of his reach now. So what is it that makes him different?

When you ask him, Blair talks about his journey as a collection of circumstances, surprises, and "accidents" that most of us would identify as familiar to our own experiences of life. He's one of the many people who, when looking back over their past, often exclaim in surprise, "How in God's name (literally) did I get here?"

But just the other day, Blair related a story that helped me understand how people like him are formed. It wasn't a story of great discernment or courage. In fact, it was a story of failure—in particular, it was a poignant story of the failure of Blair's faith. This story unlocks a bit of the mystery of how an ordinary disciple like Blair ends up doing extraordinary things in God's name.

In his work supervising IJM's offices in South Asia, Blair

travels frequently to work alongside our colleagues there. Several weeks ago, he was working with one of the offices that had carefully planned an operation on a local brick kiln where the owner held several individuals as slaves. A careful investigation had been conducted and six victims identified—three who had escaped and sought protection from the violent kiln owner, and three more who were still trapped inside. The victims' stories were documented in painstaking detail. Relevant sections of the law were cited to remove any question as to whether the victims were slaves fully deserving emancipation and restitution. Local authorities were approached and made aware of the situation. An agreement was reached and a date was set for an operation on the establishment to remove the victims from the kiln and to arrest the perpetrators. A veteran of at least fifty such operations, Blair was riding along to lend advice, help, and support to the team, some of whose members were new IJM staff.

The first part of the operation seemed to go well. As the local magistrate and IJM team entered the brick kiln, the victims were easily identified. And almost immediately, the magistrate questioned them in order to confirm their status as bonded labor slaves—a good sign. Over the years, Blair had learned to move this early stage of the operation along as quickly as possible. The longer it takes, the greater the chance the perpetrators can get word to their friends, sometimes resulting in crowds gathering around the facility. Crowds can quickly become mobs, and IJM staff have been beaten and threatened in the midst of such throngs in the past. But so far, no crowd gathered at the brick kiln.

The team encountered its first operational snag, however, when another government official arrived at the kiln. This official was known to Blair's team. On a previous operation, this man had been hostile both to IJM staff and the victims they sought to rescue. This same official aggressively inserted himself into the questioning already underway, bogging down the entire process.

What followed was a confusing and bizarre turf battle as the two officials seemed to fight for control of the investigation. An inspection of the kiln was called for, as well as a demonstration of the brick-making process. The frightened victims complied with the officials' commands, while all along Blair and the IJM team watched more and more time go by.

Eventually the six victims were all removed to the office of the local magistrate, the government official with the authority and responsibility to determine the slaves' right to be set free. It is the magistrate who issues each victim's release certificate—a personal Emancipation Proclamation—declaring that person's legal freedom and right to restitution under a government program. This new freedom and release also signals the survivor's enrollment into IJM's two-year aftercare program.[1]

It was at the office of the magistrate that a crowd began to gather. Before the inquiry could be completed, almost fifty people howed up. Most appeared to be in league with the brick kiln owner. As is usually the case, there was a lot of yelling and some pushing. There are two things that happen in these situations. First there is an electric sense of insecurity and fear that radiates through the crowd, turning an already chaotic situation into a potentially explosive one. Second, there is an almost imperceptible pendulum that swings back and forth as the powerful brick kiln owners and their friends try to influence the magistrate's decision. The simple goal of such a mob is to create enough of a tug-of-war between rule of law and rule of power that the slave owner can convince the magistrate to disregard the clear standard of the law and order all the victims back into captivity.

Standing in the middle of the chaos, Blair experienced a flood of different feelings. As the veteran, he was there to instill confidence in both the IJM employees and the government officials, all of whom had significantly less experience with these operations. As the veteran, it was his job to give clear direction to the IJM staff and determined advocacy on the victims' behalf to encourage the magistrate to do the right thing. And as the veteran—and one of just a few obviously foreign faces—Blair found himself the lightning rod for the crowd's anger. Blair was all too aware of the power of a crowd. The outcome of such operations is never secure, and often the scales of justice hang on the thinnest of threads.

As the futures of the six children and adults removed from the facility teetered back and forth, Blair felt he should pray. Clearly God cared about each of the victims. Clearly God was concerned about the safety of the staff under Blair's care. But in this moment, pushed to the limit as he was, Blair's faith reached a failure point: he found himself incapable of the faith such prayer would require. The faith muscle he needed so desperately was exhausted at the very instant he needed it most. In his paralysis, Blair sent an e-mail to his IJM colleagues in Washington, DC— an urgent call for prayer.

I remember this message being relayed to us during our daily staff prayer meeting. We prayed for the safety of Blair and his team. We prayed for the safety of those who had been removed from the kiln. We prayed that the magistrate would have the courage to do the right thing and release the slaves.

Muscle Failure

As I grow older, one of the things I find hard to live with is the inevitable loss of physical strength. I am by no means feeble (yet), but for much of my life I've taken for granted my healthy, strong back and the ability it affords me to lift heavy things. As I work my way through my forties, there is a perceptible loss of muscle mass that seems inversely proportional to the weight gain I've experienced during the same period. The result is a slow, seemingly inexorable settling of the body into middle age.

Recently I decided to try to begin counteracting this process. My ten-year-old son, Aidan, and I began a fitness program that includes both aerobic exercise and weight lifting. Doing this together has been a delight. At the beginning especially, there was painful stiffness and soreness, but the discomfort was soon overcome by the surprising joy of doing this crazy program together.

I was particularly interested in the weight lifting aspect of our program. The literature I'd read promised that while loss of muscle mass was inevitable, it could be counteracted with hard work. New to me was the idea that the goal in strength training is to push your muscles to the failure point. It is a simple process. You start an exercise with a comfortable level of weight at a higher number of repetitions, then progressively increase the weight and decrease the repetitions until essentially the muscle group you are exercising fails.

It's fascinating. One minute you can lift the weight; the next minute you can't. You can watch it happen. Your brain tells your muscles to lift, and a weight that under normal circumstances would be no problem at all goes up slowly, stops about halfway, hovers for a moment, then floats back down and you are spent.

What was new for me about this process was the idea that this "failure point" is the very thing that induces muscle growth. In the days following the exertion, the muscles actually *grow*—they recover and are more ready for the next challenge. In fact, if we don't push to the point of failure, we will find our results significantly decreased.

I believe the same thing is true of faith.

One perspective on what happened for Blair that day at the

magistrate's office in South Asia was that he failed. In a moment when he was called on to offer leadership and support to younger and less experienced staff, he fell short. And perhaps there is some truth to this perspective. But I think there is a much deeper story, one that helps explain who Blair has become as a courageous follower of Jesus. What happened that day for Blair is something that has undoubtedly happened for him many times before: his faith muscle simply reached the failure point. At the very point when he needed to exercise faith, he found himself incapable. God's power to act remained unaffected by Blair's faith, but Blair's ability to trust in God was simply depleted, exhausted.

If faith can be compared to a muscle, then Blair is someone who exercises it more than most of us. The very nature of the work he's chosen dictates that he is likely to hit failure points like these with some regularity. And if faith, like a muscle, grows best when it's been pushed to the failure point, then perhaps this offers some meaningful explanation for how Blair has become who he is today. Perhaps the steady exercise and growth of Blair's faith offers some perspective on why a challenging call to leave a life of safety and security to step out into a world of risk and uncertainty is something that Blair has wholeheartedly accepted. Blair came to IJM already familiar with what it looks and feels like to push one's faith to the failure point. He is a testimony to the truth that when faith is tested and pushed—especially to the failure point—it can recover stronger and more ready for the next challenge.

The resolution to Blair's story was not simple or quick. Eventually the crowd around his team dispersed. In DC we continued to pray, but resolution was slow to come. In the end, however, the magistrate did the right thing. All six slaves were given official certificates of freedom and enrolled in IJM's aftercare program.

Looking back, of course, it's much easier to see that God was the one in control. God was "on the hook" for the success or failure of this operation. When we look into the Scriptures, we see that God was and is much more deeply concerned about each of these men and women than Blair or the rest of our IJM staff could have ever been. Blair reaching his failure point had no impact on God's willingness to act. Blair finding himself unable to muster the strength to pray did not limit God's willingness to rescue. Blair gave it his all. He left it all out on the field. The miracle was God's responsibility.

Discipleship at the Failure Point of Faith

For most of us, learning to do anything requires the willingness to fail. An *un*willingness to fail can be a significant barrier to learning. Gifted students are seldom limited by intellect; what undoes them most often is fear of failure. Why should it be any surprise that the same is true of faith? Any significant growth in faith will require risk and even failure. Understandably, this is uncomfortable. Especially as we get older, we become used to being successful and in control. Over time our comfort zone shrinks to encompass little more than the things we are good at and endeavors at which we can reasonably expect success.

God's gracious call to us is an invitation to pursue him out of our comfort zones and into a place where failure is a real possibility—perhaps even an inevitability. It's a call to follow God to places where dependence on him is a *necessity*. Because he loves us, God invites us into his work in the world. And if we accept, we will face problems so big, situations so complex, suffering so profound, evil so real and palpable that our faith in God will hit its failure point on a regular basis. But to shrink back from this invitation is to accept a lesser, weaker version of faith. To accept this invitation is to discover that the work of justice is significantly about our own discipleship.

Questions to Consider

- What do you think of the concept of the failure point?
- As you look back over your faith journey, when have you experienced significant periods of growth? How are these periods of growth related to risk?
- Have you ever experienced a failure point in your faith? If so, what was that like?
- What are the kinds of challenges that are most likely to lead you to the failure point?

Snap here with your smartphone or visit the link to reflect with Jim on the surprising benefits of hitting your own failure point.

www.tyndal.es/JustChurch1

CHAPTER 2

The Nature of Faith

For truly I tell you, if you have faith the size of a mustard seed, you will say to this mountain, "Move from here to there," and it will move; and nothing will be impossible for you.   MATTHEW 17:20

WHEN I WAS TEN years old, my family moved to Spain for a year. It was my first experience of the look and feel, the culture and cuisine of a new and very different place. The experience shaped me in lots of important ways. It also left me with an enduring love for Spanish food. Over the last few years, I've become enamored of recreating some of the foods I grew to love during my year there. One of the classic dishes in this category is, of course, paella. Like many classic Spanish dishes, a basic paella is a simple combination of just a few ingredients: rice, seafood, and a handful of vegetables. Other than these ingredients, the dish is flavored with a single spice—saffron.

Saffron itself is fascinating. Prized for its qualities as both a spice and a coloring agent, it has been traded for thousands of years. Saffron is not made; it is harvested from flowers. When a certain type of crocus flower is in bloom, delicate inner structures of the flower (stigmas and styles) are carefully plucked by hand. These deep-maroon, threadlike parts are then dried. Because of the difficulty related to cultivating and harvesting saffron, it is by far the most expensive of all spices—more expensive, pound for pound, than gold. Fortunately, a little bit goes a long way. Just a small pinch of saffron crushed with a mortar and pestle will season a paella large enough to feed a dozen people. It doesn't just infuse the dish with its telltale bright yellow color; it imparts a heady, earthy aroma and a flavor that leaves a deep impression on both your palate and your memory.

According to Jesus, faith is like that. Like a mustard seed, or perhaps a saffron thread, a little bit goes a long way and leaves a lasting impression. But what *is* faith?

In the dictionary, the word *faith* is usually assigned two categories of definition. The first category has to do with the concept of *belief.* This is likely the kind of definition that first comes to mind for us when we think of the word *faith*, and perhaps rightly so. But the concept of belief alone does not fully convey the meaning of the word *faith.* The second half of the definition of *faith* has to do with the concept of *trust.* I'll expand more on these ideas below, but for now, perhaps we can generalize each half of the definition this way:

Belief: deciding that what we know about God is really true

Trust: deciding it's safe to act on the above beliefs

A simple way to summarize it might be the following equation:

Faith = Belief + Trust

Faith is composed of both things.

If you spend a little time reflecting on your own experience, you'll likely come to the conclusion (as I did) that most churches do something of a lopsided job teaching the two components of the faith equation. For two thousand years the church has been working hard to teach belief to its members. And to its credit, the church continues to excel at that teaching to this day. Most of the work we do as a church has to do with teaching belief. It's understandable because not only is belief very important, it is so much easier to teach than trust. Belief can be reduced to doctrine and creed. So we have Sunday school classes for new believers, seminars on church doctrine, and graduate courses that teach systematic theology. We are (and should be) continually digging deeper into what we know to be true about God. But good theology and sound doctrine, as important as they are, are only half of the task.

Growing in trust is the other half of the equation. And trust is a concept much harder to teach and much harder to learn. The biggest obstacle in learning how to trust for most of us living in the "developed" world is the very pattern of our lives. Our day-to-day existence simply doesn't require much trust of us—or much faith, for that matter. In my experience, this is true in large part because the problems we encounter in our daily lives are not very significant. In fact, most of our problems (with a few notable exceptions) fall into the category of frustrations or annoyances rather than problems.

On Frustrations and Ocean Sunfish

I remember being fascinated by the ocean sunfish during a trip to the Monterey Bay Aquarium several years ago. If you've never seen one up close, you are missing out. They inspire dumbfounded gazes from those encountering them for the first time. Their shape is not entirely unlike the small freshwater sunfish

I used to catch as a kid at a local pond with my brothers. But their scope is entirely different.

An ocean sunfish, like other fish, has a defensive strategy to protect itself from would-be predators. The freshwater sunfish has a set of sharp spines protruding from its dorsal fin to ward off hungry fish. Other ocean fish, like the blowfish, can quickly inflate to several times their original size. The ocean sunfish, a benign and docile creature, has an ingenious defensive strategy to ensure it is not eaten by other sea creatures: it *grows*. It grows so rapidly and to such an enormous size that it has few natural predators. The average adult sunfish weighs over two tons (though some adults have been known to weigh significantly more). But it's not just the size of the fish that makes its growth an effective defense mechanism; it's the unnatural rate at which it grows. The specimen I viewed at the aquarium had grown from 57 to 880 pounds in just fifteen months. That's an average weight gain of almost two pounds per day!

The net result of all this growth is a fish that is more spectacle than animal. To say it is big somehow isn't enough; it's grotesquely huge. The proportions of its parts do not match the scale of the animal as a whole. The combination of the ocean sunfish's ability to grow gigantic quickly and reproduce prolifically (females can produce as many as three hundred *million* eggs at a time) have effectively ensured its survival.

Perhaps I was particularly captivated by the ocean sunfish during that visit because I'd been reflecting on a couple of rapidly growing frustrations in my own life. One simply had to do with the feeling that I'd been underappreciated by the ministry I'd been working for. I had recently been passed over for a leadership position I was interested in and felt quite qualified for. What was amazing to me was just how quickly this frustration grew in size to take over so much of the focus of my life. I thought about it more than I feel comfortable admitting. A lot of my energy was consumed as I worked through the frustrations that seemed to reproduce prolifically into other areas of my life.

Around the same time, my wife and I were building a house. Because of my flexible ministry schedule, I was able to do much of the work myself. As the house approached a state of completion that would allow us to move in, a series of delays cropped up having to do with contractors. It's a familiar story, by no means unique to me. But what is remarkable, again, is how quickly and completely these frustrations took over almost all my conscious thought. They grew and reproduced with a rapidity that ensured they would last for a long time.

Inevitably, when I voiced these frustrations, well-meaning friends would share encouragement and Scripture with me. One passage that came up with rather annoying frequency was the first few verses of James:

> My brothers and sisters, whenever you face trials of any kind, consider it nothing but joy, because you know that the testing of your faith produces endurance; and let endurance have its full effect, so that you may be mature and complete, lacking in nothing.
> JAMES 1:2-4

I've always considered this a challenging passage. In the midst of significant life frustrations, here is James offering his difficult reframing perspective. Seemingly—and this always appeared a tired cliché to me—we should learn to see these challenges as opportunities. Counterintuitively, we will find in them the surprising presence of God bringing us to maturity *through* rather than *in spite of* the challenges. This has always been one of those ideas much easier to apply in the abstract than in reality.

Somehow I muddled my way through the vocational and

home-building challenges. But I remained perplexed about this passage until it dawned on me one day that the people James was writing to were living a drastically different kind of life than I was. Their lives were full of drastically different challenges than my own. They had real problems.

A Church with Real Problems

James opens his letter this way: "James, a servant of God and of the Lord Jesus Christ, to the twelve tribes in the Dispersion: Greetings" (James 1:1). *The twelve tribes in the Dispersion?* As I think back over the (at this point brief) history of the new church that began at Pentecost, the story begins to take shape. It's worth walking through the first few chapters of the book of Acts to help us understand the mind-set of the members of the early church. Understanding the perspective of the author's original audience will make these first few verses of James clearer. What would they have understood James to be saying? Why were they dispersed? What trials were they facing?

At the beginning of the book of Acts, the disciples are together in Jerusalem, obeying Jesus' command to wait for the promised Holy Spirit—who eventually arrives with the promised power Jesus refers to in Acts 1. As this power begins to manifest itself in Acts 2, a crowd gathers to jeer and marvel at Jesus' strange band of followers. The people watching don't quite know what to make of the fact that while people of different cultures and languages are all listening to the disciples talk, the listeners hear the disciples speaking in their own languages. Peter takes advantage of the opportunity to address the crowd.

Going all the way back to the prophet Joel and even further, Peter explains at some length and with characteristic directness that the recently crucified Jesus is the long-awaited Lord and Messiah.

Those within earshot are cut to the heart and ask what they should do. Peter says they should repent and be baptized so they, too, can receive the Holy Spirit. The result of this first day of ministry is that the church grows instantly from about 120 beleaguered and mourning souls to over 3,000 brand-new believers. Everyone seems to be filled with awe at what God is doing (and what God is capable of). This leads to radical generosity with possessions, food, time, and wealth to the extent that (not surprisingly) new people are added to this family of faith every day.

Sometime later, Peter and John heal a paraplegic at the Beautiful Gate on the way to prayer in the Temple. As a result, this new community hits its first bump in the road. Peter, again concerned that those who witnessed the healing might misunderstand this new power the apostles seem to be wielding, preaches another quite direct sermon. The Temple leadership is "much annoyed" that Peter and John are teaching that "in Jesus there is the resurrection of the dead" (Acts 4:2). (It's quite possible they were also annoyed and perhaps frightened that this new band of Jesus-followers now numbered about five thousand.) So Peter and John are summarily thrown into prison overnight.

The next day there is a kind of inquest. All of the important Temple leaders are there. It seems the main purpose of the proceeding is to bully Peter and John into no longer teaching or healing in the name and power of Jesus of Nazareth. Peter and John are not intimidated. In fact, they are so courageous and eloquent that the panel of leaders takes special note that these otherwise normal, uneducated men had been "companions of Jesus" (Acts 4:13). And far from being able to impose a gag rule on these men, the Temple leaders themselves are mute in the face of the once-lame man standing right in front of them, a walking example of the transforming power to which Peter and John seem to have access.

It's interesting to note that this event produces celebration when Peter and John finally return home and are among friends. This first experience of trouble with the authorities only *increases* the community's faith. Chapter 4 closes with another picture of radical generosity and concern for the vulnerable in the community. Members of means in the community sell some of their abundance and place the proceeds at the feet of the apostles to provide for everyone as they have need.

By this time the word is out. It is generally accepted that this group in Jerusalem is so purposeful and united that Luke borrows a political term—*ecclesia*, historically used to describe citizens called together as a legislative assembly—to describe the followers of Jesus. The believers are a group of citizens—not of Rome, but of another Kingdom—who have been called out for a purpose. This is the first time the word we have come to understand as "church" is used in this context.

But as the purpose and power of this community becomes clear, the opposition to it intensifies. A larger coalition of Jewish leaders, "filled with jealousy" (Acts 5:17), arrests the apostles and throws them into prison. This time, the prison doors are secretly and miraculously opened during the night. And unbeknownst to the Temple leadership, the apostles are dispatched to the Temple by an angel of the Lord, who instructs them to "tell the people the whole message about this life" (Acts 5:20).

A somewhat comic scene arises the next morning as the officials arrive at court for the proceedings. It's easy to imagine the people of importance filing in: the high priest and his entourage, the Sadducees, and the whole body of elders of Israel. They settle in, and at last they send for the wretched prisoners. A dumbfounded Temple police returns to report that everything in the prison is normal—doors locked, guards in their places, nothing at all unusual—except there are no prisoners inside! Just as everyone wonders what could possibly have happened, a messenger announces that the very people who were supposed to be in custody for preaching are at this very moment in the Temple court—preaching!

After rounding up the offenders yet again, the religious leaders try once more to extract a promise that the apostles will desist from their teaching. The apostles again decline, saying there's a higher authority they must obey. On the advice of the respected Gamaliel, the body of leaders decides to let this new *ecclesia* run its course—at least for now. They order the apostles (again) not to speak any more in Jesus' name. This time, however, the apostles are beaten before they are released. Oddly enough, this beating produces *joy*. The apostles *rejoice* because they are considered worthy to suffer such dishonor for the sake of Jesus.

By the time we get to chapter 6, the extravagant growth of the church has caused logistical issues. As recipients of the community's generosity, some of the widows feel they are being slighted in the daily distribution of food. Particularly concerning is the realization that the slighted widows all belong to the same ethnic group.[1] The apostles quickly and justly arrive at a solution. They invite the aggrieved ethnic group to select seven spiritually mature and wise candidates from among themselves to oversee the distribution of food to the entire community. Among them is a young man named Stephen.

It quickly becomes clear that Stephen does not limit himself to the distribution of food. He is soon recognized as a leader and speaker among the community. The jealous machinations of a local sect result in Stephen being called before a council of Temple leaders on trumped-up charges. The high priest, who undoubtedly has a long list of questions and his own speech prepared, only manages to ask Stephen one question. Stephen's answer encompasses almost the entirety of chapter 7. His clear review of Old Covenant history and his passionate assertion that the current tribunal is in the same prophet-killing spirit as ancient Israel so enrages the council that they drag Stephen out of the city and immediately stone him at the approving feet of an up-and-coming Pharisee named Saul.

Chapter 8 begins with these words: "That day a severe persecution began against the church in Jerusalem, and all except the apostles were scattered throughout the countryside of Judea and Samaria" (Acts 8:1). It is to these scattered people in this state of shock and mourning at the murder of Stephen that James writes, "My brothers and sisters, whenever you face trials of any kind, consider it nothing but joy" (James 1:2). Far from concerns about promotions at work, far from frustrations over contractors delaying the kitchen remodel, the trials James refers to are life-and-death issues—literally. For those dispersing from Jerusalem, living life as followers of Jesus has become *dangerous*.

Reading through the story of the early church, I had to acknowledge that the lives my friends and I were living were drastically different from the lives of those called out to be the church of the first century.

For this early Christian community, the trials of daily life had to do with being called before an inquest, being beaten, seeing one of their friends stoned to death, witnessing state-sponsored terror meted out against their community simply because of their faith—what they believed *and* trusted. And somehow in the midst of this, they experienced God powerfully on the move. Part of considering it all joy must have had to do with the tremendous privilege of seeing God come through in places, at times, and in ways where nothing short of miraculous intervention would have saved the day. Perhaps the joy had to do with being present at the dramatic rescue, welcoming thousands into the family of faith, seeing the miraculous healing with their own eyes. These experiences grow faith and cause disciples to mature.

What James wrote can be reduced to a simple equation for maturing faith: trials produce joy because eventually we learn that testing results in endurance, which produces maturity. And it is clear from the context of James that this maturity has a *missional* purpose. It is not just maturity for maturity's sake. In the mind of James, this process produces maturity for the purpose of courageous love and service to others. With his focus on being hearers and *doers* of the Word (see James 1:22-26) and his assertion that works are the necessary companion to and evidence of faith (see James 2:14-26), clearly James is talking about a maturity grounded in missional action: obedience.

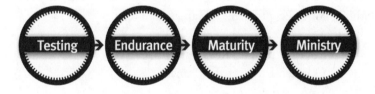

But I have to confess that often this is just not my reality. Often I find myself completely occupied by run-of-the-mill frustrations that have grown and reproduced with the unnatural speed of ocean sunfish. And all too often they grow until they become grotesquely huge and fully occupy all of the available space in my life. And while my frustrations are effective at consuming all of my available time and energy, these trials don't get me very far into the maturation process. Far from producing endurance or maturity, these small trials breed only more frustration.

Looking for Trouble

I've come to realize that the only trials that tend to come my way are trials of the mundane sort I mentioned earlier. Left to my own designs, I am doomed to repeat the cycle of having "trials" like slow Internet service or a mistaken charge on my cell phone bill consume me. And I don't think this problem is limited to me. I find that many of my friends are consumed in the same way by trials that, while being real in their own way, pale in comparison to the sort of trials James referred to. And more to the point, these small trials never really deliver on the joy that James talks about.

And because our trials aren't producing that kind of joy, many of us turn inward and resort to reexamining the quality of our worship. Perhaps another church with another worship style will help. Perhaps more expository preaching on Sunday will change our experience of God during the week. The way I read Scripture, this is not a new problem; it is an ancient one:

> Hear, O my people, and I will speak,
>   O Israel, I will testify against you.
>   I am God, your God.
> Not for your sacrifices do I rebuke you;
>   your burnt offerings are continually before me.
> I will not accept a bull from your house,
>   or goats from your folds.
> For every wild animal of the forest is mine,
>   the cattle on a thousand hills.
> I know all the birds of the air,
>   and all that moves in the field is mine.
>
> If I were hungry, I would not tell you,
>   for the world and all that is in it is mine.

Do I eat the flesh of bulls,
    or drink the blood of goats?
Offer to God a sacrifice of thanksgiving,
    and pay your vows to the Most High.
Call on me in the day of trouble;
    I will deliver you, and you shall glorify me.

PSALM 50:7-15

Clearly God is upset here. There is some issue that needs to be clarified. Israel has been focused on the act of sacrifice in a misguided way. Somehow they have come to the mistaken conclusion that the bulls and wheat are to be sacrificed because God *needs* something from them. This could not be further from the truth. With a touch of sarcasm, God quips, "If I were hungry, I would not tell you." God owns the cattle on a thousand hills! It's not the sacrifices themselves, but the people's understanding of their importance that needs to change.

Cain and Abel's story had made clear that in the case of offerings, the better sacrifice involves the firstfruits of the harvest or the "firstlings" of the flock (see Genesis 4:2-5). For an agrarian society, these firstfruits represent something important: security. For a farmer, the best 10 percent of the harvest would likely be kept as seed for the next year's crop. Similarly, animal sacrifices were to be specimens without blemish sacrificed in the prime of their lives. To a herder, these animals represent breed stock. They are the gene pool from which you want to build the rest of your herd or flock. In this way, the sacrificial system consistently required those in it to sacrifice their security.

A large flock and a good harvest would be tempting places to find security for your future. You might even be tempted to build bigger and bigger barns to hold the great blessing of the abundant harvest (Luke 12:13-21). But this misses a vital and central point: There is nothing you can do to ensure your own security. True security comes only as a gift from God. In the Old Testament, I find that God is most angered and frustrated when his people try to set up their lives in a way that makes faith (in the sense of *trust* in God's provision) unnecessary. This tendency is both ancient and very modern.

God's remedy is found in Psalm 50. What does God really want of us? It's pretty simple: "Call on me in the day of trouble; I will deliver you, and you shall glorify me" (Psalm 50:15). What is the right relationship between God and his people? We call on God when we are in trouble, and he rescues us. In some ways, the whole sacrificial system is one big reminder that we need to live life in such a way that we are *aware* of our dependence on God. Our awareness doesn't change anything but our responsiveness to his presence and work around us. God is present regardless, but we run the risk of missing this truth. When are we most aware of God's presence and work? I'm most aware of God—and most responsive to him—when I am in trouble. It's so simple, I find it almost humorous. But clearly what God wants of us is to call on him in the day of trouble. So here's the formula for right relationship with God according to Psalm 50:

Step 1: Get into trouble.

Step 2: Call out to God.

Step 3: God rescues.

Step 4: God is glorified.

Finding Your Voice

My colleague Pranitha Timothy knows exactly what trouble looks like. And she didn't have to go looking for it. The daughter of dedicated missionary doctors, she grew up in a tiny village in rural India. Trouble came and found Pranitha as she observed the plight of the poor in her village and in the rock quarries, brick kilns, and rice mills that surrounded it. From a tender age, Pranitha understood that the very poor in India have just one job: to toil all day long while those around them don't seem to notice or care.

Her parents' dedication to serve the poor left its impression on her. And so Pranitha chose to pursue a career in social work. But after she received her master's degree, trouble came and found her again in the form of cancerous brain tumors that, while sparing her life, threatened to leave her without a voice. The doctor performing her surgery predicted that, while she would survive, she would likely end up physically weak and mute. But the voice inside her would not be silenced. In the midst of her trouble, Pranitha cried out to God—not just for her own rescue, but for the rescue of the vulnerable people she hoped to serve.

And God has been glorified.

Today Pranitha serves as the director of aftercare in IJM's field office in Chennai, India—a team that is dedicated to bringing rescue to victims of forced labor. The miracle of her own rescue has instilled her with a kind of courage, perseverance, and hope that is utterly remarkable. As of this writing, Pranitha has led her team in bringing rescue and restoration to nearly four thousand children, women, and men once held as slaves in brick kilns, rock quarries, and rice mills in her region of India. Pranitha herself will tell you, "My struggle with cancer has left me with a strange voice. But God has used it as a voice for the voiceless." Clearly Pranitha has been shaped—by trouble—into the heroic and courageous person God created her to be. Trouble came and found her. She cried out to God. God rescued her. And God was glorified.

But what about us? How do we enter into this process? How

do we say yes to what James is offering? How do we grow in maturity into disciples capable of great faith?

Over the years, the shorthand term I've begun using for this process is *looking for trouble*. The fact that my life is so different from those of first-century Christians, so insulated from the issues and challenges they faced, is significant. But, as Pranitha saw, it doesn't have to be limiting. The world is still much the same as it was then, even if the part of it where I live is quite isolated and sanitized. "Looking for trouble" is about making the concrete decision to emerge from our isolation. It's about deciding to peel back some of the layers of our insulation so that we begin to experience the world as it really is. Once we open the door to the reality and scope of injustice-related suffering in our world, our hearts will be plenty troubled. It may not sound easy, but there are some very simple ways this can be done.

It's Like Learning to Ride a Bike

A friend once told me that the fastest way to teach a child to ride a bike is to take off the training wheels. Learning to ride a bike, after all, is about learning *not* to fall. With the training wheels on, falling is almost impossible. The fastest way to teach a child, my friend suggested, is to take off the training wheels and to run alongside the child, holding only the seat of the bicycle. The object, he insisted, is not to hold the bike steady but rather to rock it gently and rhythmically back and forth—to keep the bicycle continually *out* of balance. Thoroughly unconvinced, I immediately forgot my friend's advice—until my oldest child, Clara, received her first two-wheeler.

At least as excited as Clara was, I quickly assembled the new bike. And without giving it a second thought, I bolted on the training wheels. My daughter loved it. With the training wheels on, she was able to ride back and forth across the sidewalk and around the school playground safely and happily, but I couldn't see any progress toward her actually learning to ride without training wheels. Every time we talked about taking the training wheels off, she would plead that she wasn't ready. This went on for several months until one fine day, I decided it was time. I gently convinced her that we should try the bike without the training wheels. I promised her I'd be right beside her the whole way. After repeated pleas for reassurance that I would not let go, she reluctantly agreed.

Up and down the sidewalk we went, Clara clinging tightly to the handlebars, squeaking continually, "Are you still holding on?" My sore back made it clear that this method wasn't working either. Instead of the training wheels, I was now doing most of the work. And as my back grew increasingly incapable of supporting the weight of Clara and her bike, the wisdom of my friend's advice suddenly struck me. I realized that what Clara needed to learn was how to keep the bike balanced on her own. Relying on me was little better than relying on the training wheels. If she wanted to ride the two-wheeler, sooner or later she would need to feel the discomfort of losing her balance in order to learn how to gain it back all by herself.

I sat her back down and carefully explained what we were going to do. I insisted that I would not let go, but that she might feel a little uncomfortable as the bike swayed back and forth slightly. She agreed to give it a try.

On the next trip up the sidewalk, I gently rocked the bicycle back and forth from one side to the other, through the balance point and across the other side. At first this was greeted with shrieks of mild panic from Clara. But as she got used to the motion, she realized that it was a simple and natural thing to correct her balance by turning the handlebars just slightly in the direction of the "fall." Within a few passes, she was easily managing the slightly swerving path of the bike. It was clear that she was more and more in control. Amazingly enough, within a few minutes, she was riding up and down the sidewalk all by herself!

Recall the basic formula I offered at the beginning of this chapter: Faith = Belief + Trust. Imagine for a minute what it would have been like if I'd tried to teach Clara how to ride her bike by simply helping her *believe* it would work. I could have sat her down in the living room and patiently explained, "You see, Clara, a two-wheeler becomes more stable the faster it goes. The spinning wheels create something called a gyroscopic force. This force creates stability along the axis of the wheels. So even though it's counterintuitive, honey, the faster you go down the sidewalk, the more stable the bicycle becomes!" As true as this is, even if she could have understood it at the time, it would not have helped her ride the bicycle.

In order to overcome the natural fear she had, she needed to develop a sense of trust that it really was safe to *act* on what I was telling her. As a loving father, I was committed to helping her learn that trust in the most comfortable way possible. But as all of us who have learned to ride a two-wheeler know, there is no way to avoid the fear of falling—the feeling of risk. And in the end, it didn't take long for Clara to trust because the principles behind the two-wheeler are sound, but it was essential for her to test those principles out and learn that they are indeed true.

Clearly, taking the training wheels off the bike was an opportunity for Clara to go looking for trouble. With the training wheels on, she was content to ride on the playground. She felt safe. But riding her bike on the playground wasn't really getting her anywhere. The same is true for us. Most of us, in order to grow in our faith, will need to learn to trust God more deeply—even in the midst of the possibility of fear and failure. The first step toward deeper trust might be to remove our training wheels. When we put ourselves in positions where we could fall, we have no choice but to depend on God.

Perhaps you are reading this book because you sense it's time to take off the training wheels, time to test the principles behind your beliefs and discover that they are sound. There are some simple ways to do this, but it will require something of you: it will require that you move beyond your frustrations and go looking for trouble. Fortunately, it can be easier than you think.

Sometimes having children is an invitation to this kind of trouble. Or choosing to seek reconciliation in a difficult marriage situation. Sometimes the choice to remain single invites this kind of trouble. Or a choice to live and minister in a difficult community. Sometimes the choice to cross the road, like the Good Samaritan, invites this kind of trouble.

One way I see people find this kind of trouble every year is at IJM's Global Prayer Gathering. In the spring of every year, IJM gathers all of our field office directors from around the world and brings them to Washington, DC. And for one weekend we invite hundreds of friends of IJM to simply come and pray for these leaders and their teams of lawyers, social workers, and investigators, as well as those they serve—the children, women, and men victimized by violent abuse. Every year I see the familiar signs of people in deep trouble. I can see it on their faces as they hear a field office director explain the dangerous places where IJM investigators are searching out victims of sex trafficking and slavery; I can hear it in their words as they engage with God, asking him to rescue victims waiting for help and to restore survivors of abuse. I see it as they pray *big* prayers—calling on God to bring an end to forced labor or to police abuse of power. To transform a city where entrenched injustice has, for years, denied the poor any hope for security. To comfort a widow who has been chased from her home. To rescue a girl hidden in a brothel network. To restore a family after decades of enslavement.

This is what I mean by *trouble*: It's the place where we have become so identified with the suffering of our neighbors that we are suffering alongside them. It's the place of desperation where we cannot help but fall at God's feet and beg for his intervention. The place where we are acutely aware that we ourselves need rescue—and the only one who can save us is God.

Questions to Consider

- What are some experiences that have matured you in the category of belief?
- What are some experiences that have matured you in the category of trust?
- Have you experienced trials that are like ocean sunfish? Explain.
- Describe a time when you called on God from a place of trouble. How did God respond? How did you respond to God?
- What might it look like for you to "take off the training wheels"?
- Have you ever gone "looking for trouble"? What did you do? What was the result?

Snap here with your smartphone or visit the link to learn what it takes for us to become more deeply trusting disciples.

www.tyndal.es/JustChurch2

CHAPTER 3

Finding Trouble in the Andes

Call on me in the day of trouble; I will deliver you, and you shall glorify me.   PSALM 50:15

IN THE LAST CHAPTER I suggested that many of our day-to-day lives are so safe that we seldom run into the kind of trouble that Psalm 50 describes—the kind of trouble where our only recourse is to call out to God for deliverance. At the same time, many of us are crying out to experience God in a way that is fresh, real, and new. The solution offered in chapter 2 is the idea of *looking for trouble.* But what does looking for trouble actually look like? What kind of trouble are we looking for? Where can we find it?

For me, these questions were answered one night around a dinner table in Saratoga, California. Gary Haugen, founder of International Justice Mission, had been invited to speak at a local church on Sunday morning, and he and I, along with a few other church leaders, had been invited to share dinner with a mutual friend that evening.

I was particularly delighted to be part of the dinner party that night. I had recently transitioned out of my campus ministry role and into the role of compassion ministries pastor at

The River, which at this point was a young church plant. In the early days there were two significant ministry thrusts at The River: great preaching and inner healing. Both found deep resonance in Silicon Valley culture, and the church grew rapidly. Its location in the epicenter of the dot-com bubble soon led the church to prayerfully consider how it ought to take responsibility for its privilege and wealth. This led to growing generosity and a deepening desire to serve the needs of the surrounding community. So in 1999, I was hired as the compassion ministries pastor to lead the charge into mercy ministry.[1]

It became obvious early on that exposure to the reality of the world outside of Silicon Valley was profoundly transformational for The River's people. While it is true that there are real spiritual, psychological, and physical needs in most educated, affluent congregations in the United States, it is also true that tending exclusively to these needs can create a myopic, overly introspective climate not conducive to deep discipleship. Like ocean sunfish, these psychological and physical needs can loom so large that there is little room for a focus on the needs outside the church. So alongside a robust healing ministry, we began to consider mercy ministry as necessary to our spiritual growth.

Our initial steps into mercy ministry were quite satisfying. Among our many early efforts were a ministry in a local jail, work in homeless shelters, the beginning of an intentional community in one of the poorest neighborhoods in our city, and a growing network of international partnerships with churches and ministries in the Two-Thirds World. As more and more people participated in these mercy ministries, our perspective as a church shifted. While there was still room for appropriate concern for our personal challenges and trials, our direct exposure to poverty in our own local context, along with our frequent forays to work alongside trusted ministry partners in the Two-Thirds World, helped put our own issues into proper perspective. It is true that being passed over for a promotion is a fundamentally different kind of trial than searching frantically up to four hours a day for enough barely potable water for your family.

These new relationships were the impetus for deeper reflection for many of us. Beyond our growing awareness of the smallness of our own lives and trials, we were also compelled to reflect on the nature and power of the gospel of Jesus. Our vision of the gospel was radically broadened, and we were perceptibly transformed as a church. In time, as members of our congregation chose to prioritize ministry over other obligations, we spun off a few nonprofits that to this day are working among the poor in our city and elsewhere in the world.

It is no exaggeration to say that in the midst of these new ministries, we experienced the presence and power of God in profound ways. One of the complications, however, was that these experiences revealed our insular and often ignorant perceptions of the nature of our world. Our isolation from the depths of evil and suffering left us unequipped to answer the persistent and difficult questions of oppression and injustice we encountered.

These experiences were troubling to us in the best of ways. Why were the people we served so vulnerable? Could anything be done to protect them *before* they were abused, or should we confine ourselves to binding up the wounds caused by abuse? Treating the symptoms of oppression, while a mercy to those suffering, does not solve their problems. What the oppressed need is for justice to roll down like water. But is that the job of the church?

It was in the midst of these reflections that I read Gary Haugen's *Good News about Injustice*. I was encouraged and challenged by the book. In particular, I was excited by Gary's challenge to the church. "The church is God's plan for ending injustice in the world," Gary often says, "and God doesn't have another plan." But Gary hadn't just laid down a challenge. The book was replete with astonishing and concrete examples of Christ-followers stepping boldly into the work of justice, literally rescuing the oppressed, setting captives free, and accomplishing the kind of community transformation that prevents the vulnerable from being abused in the first place.

Since reading the book, I'd been looking for a way to connect with IJM. So when the opportunity arose to attend this dinner, I immediately cleared my schedule. It turned out that Gary and a few other IJM staff had just returned from a visit to Peru, where they had been connecting with their casework partners Paz y Esperanza (Peace and Hope). Paz y Esperanza is a Peruvian group of Christian lawyers, pastors, and psychologists who had become aware of an epidemic of child sexual abuse along the foothills of the Andes in northeastern Peru. As far back as the 1980s, they had sought to be a presence for justice amidst the abuses of the Fujimori administration and the guerilla organization known as Shining Path. Since then, the work of Paz y Esperanza has expanded throughout Peru and into Ecuador. With excellence, Paz y Esperanza seeks justice for vulnerable people across several different casework types—including sexual violence against minors.[2] IJM and Paz y Esperanza, realizing the similarity of their missions, had begun working together in Peru. Over dinner Gary and the other IJM staff took the time to paint a picture for me. They talked not just of the astonishing level of victimization, but in compelling terms they described the commitment of these Christians to actually engage this challenging issue. I was intrigued.

I called IJM the next day. I asked if there was any way that a church like The River could get involved in this work in Peru. I offered our services for the most mundane tasks—we'd be willing to carry suitcases, translate, anything!

A few months later I found myself in Huánuco, Peru, with an

IJM lawyer and a small team of lawyers and medical professionals from The River, just seven of us in all. What had gotten me there initially was a vague sense that a real connection to the work of justice would be good for our church. What I experienced was deeper and more life-altering than I could have imagined.

Trouble on the Horizon

One of the first things the Peruvian staff did was orient us to the nature and scope of the problem in Huánuco. I remember learning that in just one week, no fewer than fifty minors had come forward to report that they had been victims of sexual abuse. The statistics were indeed daunting, but the staff of Paz y Esperanza were mounting a holistic intervention involving investigators, lawyers, psychologists, and pastors. At about the midpoint of our visit, the legal staff in Huánuco took the time to walk us through four of their current cases. I remember this meeting vividly. I was tired from travel, I was mentally exhausted from speaking Spanish all day, and I was looking forward to getting back to the hotel to rest. Nevertheless, I braced myself for the meeting as Richard, the Peruvian lead lawyer, pulled out a small stack of four case files. To this day I don't remember what was in the other three files. I was so completely wrecked by the first that I have no specific recollection of the rest of the meeting.

"Let me begin with a recent case," said Richard. "We first became aware of Marta's situation just two weeks ago . . ."

Before I relate Marta's[3] story, let me explain that lawyers are trained to deal with facts. They see a case as a linkage of facts leading to possible conclusions. And so it was as a series of facts, a logical progression, that Richard presented Marta's story. Let me also warn you that this story was difficult for me to hear, and it may be difficult to read. If you or someone you love is a survivor of sexual violence, please understand that this story may trigger traumatic feelings or difficult memories for you. You may want to consider skipping ahead to page 40, or having a trusted friend read this section first.

Marta (now age eleven) and her younger brother had lived with their father in a small house outside Huánuco, Richard told me. Their trouble began several years before when Marta's mother left the family, citing repeated abuse from Marta's father. By the time she turned eight, Marta herself had become the target of unwanted attention from her father. The first time he sexually abused her was late at night, in the room she shared with her little brother. When Marta tried to resist her father, he slapped, hit, and overpowered her. He also threatened her, frightening her into silence, so that as the abuse continued—for more than a year—she was unable to speak to anyone. With no one to turn to and no one to advocate for her, Marta soon found herself trapped in a house where she was repeatedly raped at the whim of her own father. Apart from the horror of having to live in this situation, what made it especially hopeless for Marta was that it seemed there was no escape. Even if she were able to muster the courage to report the abuse, she would just trade one difficult and dangerous situation for another. If she denounced her father, her nightmare might get considerably worse. Reporting the crime would put her life in danger. And Marta was only a child. Where could she go? How would she feed and care for herself? And what of her little brother? Seeing no way out, Marta resigned herself to the nightmare. But as the abuse wore on, Richard said, Marta experienced deep trauma—both physical and emotional.

Richard relayed this part of the story accurately and efficiently. As he talked, he pulled a picture of Marta from the case file and placed it on the table.

Marta reported that about a year later, her father began a relationship with another woman who subsequently moved into their home. At first, the presence of a new stepmom seemed to improve Marta's situation. Her father's late-night visits stopped, and as Marta put it, he haunted her only in her dreams. But the new stepmother had brought with her a sixteen-year-old son, and Marta reported that it was not long before the stepson began to rape her. This stepbrother threatened to beat Marta with a stick and whip her with cords should she reveal the abuse she was suffering.

It may seem impossible, Richard continued, but the nightmare worsened. Tragically, not long after the arrival of her stepmom and stepbrother, Marta's younger brother died—the result of a bullet wound that killed him instantly. And in addition to being overwhelmed with grief, Marta was plagued by suspicion: the gun in question belonged to Marta's stepbrother, who alleged that the young boy had shot himself accidentally while playing with it. Marta knew her little brother had been aware of the abuse. She couldn't help but wonder if he had been killed to maintain the silence her father and stepbrother insisted on.

As he related this part of the story, Richard laid another photo on the table. It depicted the body of Marta's little brother.

Statistics are one thing; seeing the pictures of Marta and her little brother made it all too possible to imagine the events that had so completely shattered their young lives. Though I couldn't have described it this way at the time, I was beginning to experience my first significant failure point. My faith, my theology, my life experience simply could not accommodate Marta's story. I wanted to unlearn what I'd just heard—to purge it from my mind. But that was impossible. I racked my brain for some comforting thought, some idea, some theological construct, some passage of Scripture that would quench the fire of emotion raging in my chest. I was uncomfortable with the level of anger I was feeling—rage, even—toward anyone who would destroy the lives of little children like the ones in the pictures before me. But at the failure point, there is no such help, no easy answer. The faith I had brought with me to Peru simply failed. It was just not rugged enough to sustain me through Marta's horrific story.

When Richard finished speaking, there was a heavy silence in the room as we all tried to assimilate the facts before us. I was so frozen by the emotions crashing through me that I remember having a hard time even formulating a question. I managed to ask something about how Richard and his colleagues had learned of Marta and what had happened in the two weeks since they had taken the case.

In his same patient, factual way, Richard explained that Marta had somehow found the courage to find her birth mother and reveal the story. Together, Marta and her mother found their way to Richard and his colleagues.

Upon hearing her story, Paz y Esperanza sprang into action. They mounted a professional investigation to corroborate the facts of the story. This investigation resulted in the case file and the photographs I had seen. What Richard went on to say absolutely astounded me. Upon completing their investigation, Richard's team took the case to the prosecutor's office. An arrest warrant was issued immediately, and the police, with Paz y Esperanza's help, successfully executed the arrest. At this very moment, the father and stepbrother sat in jail, awaiting trial. While the investigative and legal work continued, Marta was enrolled in an aftercare program, where she was introduced to other survivors her age and where she began a healing process under the care of a trained psychologist.

Direct comparisons of this sort are seldom a good idea, but at the time I couldn't help but think, *What have I accomplished in the last two weeks?*

By the time the meeting was over, it was dark. A taxi brought the rest of the team from The River back to the hotel. Desperately needing to sort some things out, I decided walking back would do me some good. As I stepped into the cool of the evening and walked down the lovely streets of Huánuco, I was hit by what in the coming years would become a familiar disconnect. The small city seemed so peaceful and so beautiful. And yet Marta's case was just one of dozens that Richard and his colleagues were working on—and hundreds they had yet to discover. The night was so cool and refreshing, and by contrast, my heart was on fire with feelings ranging from rage to despair. But my confused emotions could accomplish little beyond the few tears streaking down my stunned face. I tried to sort it all out, but it would not be sorted—at least not during a forty-five-minute walk. Sorting it out, inasmuch as it could be done at all, would take years.

The writer of Hebrews says something fascinating in chapter 13. He must have understood that humans have a tendency to process the suffering of others in the abstract, to safely insulate themselves from the pain other people are experiencing. Hebrews 13:3 says, "Remember those who are in prison, as though you were in prison with them; those who are being tortured, as though you yourselves were being tortured." I'd always thought of it as a mental exercise, a process by which I would try to come to some understanding of what it must be like for those who are suffering violence. But this was no mental exercise. This was no abstraction. I had seen the photographs. I had been with Richard, who had recorded Marta's statement and witnessed her grief firsthand. And there was no chance I was going to be able to insulate myself from Marta's suffering ever again—and I didn't want to. In the Psalm 50 sense, I was in trouble. I was neck-deep in trouble, and I was having a hard time getting out.

During that walk home, I called out to God in a way I seldom had before. I wanted the situation in Huánuco changed wholesale, and I wanted it done instantly. I didn't want anyone else to suffer the way Marta had. I didn't have the power to do any of the things I wanted done. I was completely at the mercy of God. If God didn't act, the situation wasn't going to change. It was too complex and too culturally entrenched even for smart, dedicated professionals like Richard and his colleagues to handle on their own.

As if that one story weren't enough to take my faith to the failure point, among the many meetings I attended during that first trip was a gathering of all the young victims who were under Paz y Esperanza's care. Doris, the lead psychologist, along with the aftercare team, had begun gathering all of the victims together for group therapy and mutual support. They referred to this group as "Tamar."[4] The Tamar group had been meeting for a year, and the staff had arranged for a celebration. They invited our team to share in an evening of games, music, and cake.

Simply walking into the room was a bit overwhelming. It was full of kids, ages eight to fifteen or so, some boys and many girls. It could have been a gathering of kids in a youth group. It could have been a group of kids gathering to do homework. Instead, what all these children had in common was that they had been raped—usually by someone very close to them.

Understandably many of them were shy, but over the course of an hour or so, they began to open up. I remember several conversations that evening. Most prominently I remember talking to one twelve-year-old girl with freckles all over her young face. (Part of what made her so memorable was that freckles are much less common on Peruvian faces. Inwardly I wondered if her freckles had made her more of a target.) During the party, I asked her questions about school and what she liked to do with her free time. Soon she relaxed and began asking me questions. "Are you married? Do you have kids? How old are they?" I had already put together that many of the girls in the room were the same age as my own daughters, but until this young girl asked how old my kids were, the connection had not been quite so visceral. She asked a few questions about what my kids like to do, what grade they are in, and so on. The familiar smiles I saw as this young girl giggled with her friends in response to each of my answers reminded me that they were all just girls—just like *my* girls. This made their suffering even less tolerable for me. They seemed to be bearing up under it quite well with the support of the psychologists, but over the course of the evening, I was coming apart.

But this is the beauty and purpose of the failure point. Clearly, I was in way over my head. No creed, no systematic theology sufficiently explained this or sufficiently quieted the angry questions tumbling through my soul. I was forced—propelled—into God's presence. At the end of my ability to explain and even understand came an invitation in the thundering silence: an invitation to trust. God was inviting me to trust that he was good. God was inviting me to trust that he loved these girls with more love than I was capable of. God was inviting me to trust that he had good news for each one of them. And in the context of the celebration that very evening, my trust was significantly deepened through a simple worship song sung by a girl named Lucena.

Lucena's story involved a local taxi driver, a "friend" of the family who had begun to sexually abuse her when she was in her early teens. Now a shy fifteen-year-old, Lucena had an infant child resulting from the abuse. The responsibility of a baby would weigh heavily on any fifteen-year-old. In Lucena's situation, the load could have been crushing.

Over the course of the evening, we played several group games. One of them was a simple variation on musical chairs. Someone produced a small wooden box filled with slips of paper. As the music played, we were to pass the box around our circle of chairs. When the music stopped, the person holding the box was to take out a slip of paper and do whatever was written on it. The Peruvians in the room seemed very familiar with this game, and it was all set up quickly. The music started and the box went around the circle. Everyone was smiling and laughing. It all seemed like great fun until the music stopped and Lucena was left holding the box. Timidly, Lucena pulled out a slip of paper and in a barely audible voice read what was printed on it: "Sing a song to the whole group."

At this point I thought, *This is a* terrible *game! Poor Lucena, who is already wounded and withdrawn, will be further scarred by this horrible experience.* Part of me felt sure I should put a stop to the whole thing for Lucena's sake. But I trusted that the psychologists in the room knew what they were doing.

Slowly Lucena stood, and with her face flushed in embarrassment, she began to sing a common Spanish worship song in little more than a whisper:

Si tuvieras fe como un grano de mostaza,
(If you had the faith of a mustard seed)

Eso lo dice el Señor,
(This is what the Lord says)

Tú le dirías a la montaña,
(You would say to the mountain)

Muévete, muévete.
(Move, move)

My sense is that most of us were sitting there listening and trying not to feel embarrassed for Lucena. But as she came to the end of the first chorus, she suddenly called out in a surprisingly strong voice, "Everyone sing with me!" Startled, we all jumped in and sang the lines. When we got to the chorus, people stood up and danced as they sang:

> *¡Y esa montaña se moverá, se moverá, se moverá!*
> (That mountain would move, move, move!)

By the second time through the chorus, the entire circle of chairs had become a conga line dancing around the room. At the end of this rousing chorus, Lucena yelled out over all our voices, "Okay, let's sing it again—and this time, just the men!"

Obediently, and with tears in my eyes, I joined with the others on the next chorus. The significance of the words we sang was not lost on me. In fact, I think in some ways they were *for* me. The song helped me to realize that mountains—vast ranges of mountains—were moving in Lucena's life. She was experiencing a kind of healing and wholeness in this extended church family that was nothing short of miraculous. I may not have had the faith to tell those mountains to move, but others in the room certainly did. And bearing witness to their faith strengthened my own.

By God's sovereign design, the repercussions of that meeting with Richard and the celebration with the Tamar group are still reverberating in my life to this day. Hitting that failure point was the beginning place for profound growth of faith in my life.

The "Asks" Are Always Bigger than You Expect

Over the course of the ten days our team was in Huánuco, it became clear to me that there were some places where our church could engage in justice ministry by supporting Paz y Esperanza. There were little projects we could take on that might in some small but significant ways make a contribution to what these heroic brothers and sisters were doing. At the end of our trip, we had a meeting to evaluate the experience and establish what possibilities existed for future partnership. I came into the meeting with my head full of small ideas. I was hopeful that we could bring a team back the next year that could engage in some way. Perhaps we could build, paint, or clean something.

During the meeting we expressed our deep thanks and appreciation to the staff for inviting us into the work. We expressed our interest in returning and supporting what they were doing in some small but specific ways. Given the level of professionalism we had seen in all the staff throughout the trip, it should not have surprised me that they came to the meeting quite prepared and were ready to make several specific "asks" of our team. First, they asked if The River would be able to support their work financially, so that they could continue to employ Doris, the full-time psychologist on the team. This was something we were excited to do, and the church has continued to do so every year since. Doris's work is vital to the healing of each and every client in Huánuco. Second, they asked if we could bring someone to Huánuco who could offer training.

"What kind of training?" we asked.

"You see," they replied, "in all of Huánuco there are only two legal medical doctors. These doctors are the only ones (by Peruvian law) who can perform the forensic medical exam to determine if a patient has suffered sexual abuse trauma. The caseloads of these two doctors are ridiculously high, and their training has been minimal."

In classic, factual, lawyerly fashion, Richard explained that the extent of the physical exam to document sexual abuse was a legal medical doctor checking to see if a girl's hymen had been ruptured—and there was no physical exam to collect evidence in the cases of male victims. He further explained why this sort of exam was woefully inadequate. What they really needed was state-of-the-art training provided by a forensic medical professional. Not only would this training help the two legal medical doctors in their work, just as important, it would raise the bar for other officials in Huánuco regarding what constituted sexual abuse. This ask was much larger and more complex than we'd expected. But we committed to see if we could find a specialist.

After we returned to the United States, one of our original team members, a nurse-practitioner named Julie, realized that she herself could gain the necessary skills to offer the training Richard and his colleagues had asked for. Over the next few months, along with her regular job at a clinic, Julie spent untold hours talking with experts, learning and preparing to offer a multiple-hour technical seminar on examination techniques for the documentation of sexual abuse trauma.

By the time The River team returned to Peru the second time, it was clear that Richard and his team had been working very hard as well. They had advertised a series of meetings for judges, prosecutors, police, psychologists, and medical professionals. By the time Julie donned her white lab coat and stood up to give her presentation—complete with over a hundred slides and illustrations—gathered before her was almost the entire public justice system in Huánuco. Julie presented her material over the course of several hours. Richard's legal team presented a clear overview of Peruvian law with respect to child sexual assault. Together these presentations went a long way toward making the case that sexual abuse is an issue that needs to be taken seriously, that there are clear methodologies for defining what it is and what it isn't, and that it is actually possible for the community to learn how to deal with it.

Along with the meetings where Julie presented, Richard's

team had also set up a one-day pastors' conference. Our very practical hope for this conference was that the pastors attending would consider their churches as the first line of defense against sexual violence. One of the church mobilization staff from IJM and I worked together to present material on biblical justice and sexual violence to a group of nearly a hundred pastors—some of whom had walked overnight to attend.

It was a joy to the team from The River to engage the issue so directly. Again we had a meeting with Richard's legal team, where they presented several current cases. Predictably, it was a hard meeting that produced now-familiar feelings of rage and despair. But by now I was also much more aware of what Richard and his team had been aware of all along: God was on the move. These stories, as much as they broke God's heart, did not catch God by surprise. Richard's team was in the day-to-day battle, but they also had the long view. They had a growing sense of confidence that over time, God really was changing the situation.

Over years of relationship with Paz y Esperanza, qualified members of The River have provided training to local prosecutors, judges, doctors, social workers, and police on topics ranging from basic sensitivity training on domestic violence and sexual abuse to more technical seminars on victim interview techniques to minimize revictimization. Most recently, The River was able to raise enough money to purchase a twenty-five-acre property outside the city of Huánuco to serve as a combination shelter and aftercare center, ensuring the maximum possible protection of survivors. We have been privileged to witness the very beginnings of a cultural shift within the church with respect to the issues of domestic violence and sexual abuse of children in Huánuco. These evils, while still present, are no longer dark secrets to God's people. Even darkness as deep as this cannot hide from the dawn.

If We Are Risk Averse, We Will Be Faith Poor

As a kid, I remember being fascinated by people who could make their ears wiggle. It seemed like magic to me. I had an uncle who enjoyed tormenting me with the fact that he could do it and I couldn't. Every time I saw him, I'd ask him to wiggle his ears, then I'd laugh and beg him to tell me the secret. One day, he finally let me in on it. There's no real secret, he said; there is a muscle on your scalp that, when it contracts, pulls your ears upward. If you stand in front of a mirror long enough, eventually you'll be able to find that particular muscle and learn how to flex it. I ran immediately to the bathroom and stared into the mirror, willing my ears to move . . . nothing. I stood there for a long time, contorting my face into all sorts of hideous shapes. Eventually I landed on one that involved the "ear muscle," and I noticed (among the many frightening things that were happening on my face) that my ears went up! With just a few more hours of practice (which was, I'm sure you'll agree, time well spent), I was able to flex that muscle alone. And by alternatively contracting and relaxing the "ear muscle," I too was able to wiggle my ears.

For years I thought of faith the same way. I imagined there was a faith muscle somewhere in me that I just needed to isolate and learn how to flex. Somehow I imagined that I could exercise it alone, regardless of what was going on in the rest of my life— that I could sit alone in a room and grow my faith. As a person who deeply values a wide variety of spiritual disciplines, I want to be clear that I don't intend to devalue any discipline that happens in solitude and quiet; I believe that solitude and quiet are woefully underutilized spiritual disciplines.

What I am saying, and what our foray into justice ministry drove home powerfully, is that we *grow* faith not by sitting alone and trying to flex our faith muscles. We grow faith by putting ourselves in situations that will require faith of us. My experience in Peru proved again and again this principle: faith grows most profoundly when it regularly encounters the failure point. And today, I think I better understand why. The sad truth is that I so seldom run into situations in my normal life that *require* faith of me. As a reasonably well-educated middle-class person, my prayer for "daily bread" is a spiritual abstraction (albeit an important one). I am seldom concerned for health, provision of any meaningful necessity, or even comfort. My life as I live it day-to-day does not really demand that I trust in God. It is a safe, predictable experience of moving from moment to moment where I seldom feel out of control or overmatched by any situation that comes my way. How does faith in God grow under such circumstances?

In reality, it is too rare an experience for me to be asked to do something I don't feel entirely competent to do. It's not that I'm unusually accomplished as a person—not at all. It's more that I gravitate toward the activities and opportunities I know I can handle, the things I'm already good at. The risk of taking on a new challenge—so familiar to most of us when we are young—loses its flavor as we age. Engaging these issues of injustice was so valuable to me precisely because every new piece of information I learned and every new ask that was made so effectively required faith of me. And this kind of faith is required whenever we take on a significant challenge or risk: a ministry opportunity at home, sharing our own faith with friends, choosing to give sacrificially in some way. This is why risk is so important. If we are risk averse, we will be faith poor.

Questions to Consider

- Spend time reading and discussing Psalm 50 with some friends. When have you "called on God in the day of trouble"? Can you identify ways God "rescued" you? How was God glorified?

- As you read Marta's story, how did you feel? Did it produce any of the characteristics of failure of faith for you? How should you respond?
- Do Marta's and Lucena's stories offer any helpful perspective to the problems you see around you right now? In what way?
- How have you seen risk produce faith in your life?
- What choices could you make this week or this month that would put you in situations that require faith of you? (Volunteer at church? Have a conversation you've been avoiding? Take a risk?)

Snap here with your smartphone or visit the link to hear Jim's thoughts on the importance of making choices that require us to trust God—and how God meets us at the edge of our comfort zones.

www.tyndal.es/JustChurch3

CHAPTER 4

Recovering from Failure

EXCITED ABOUT THE CONCEPT of muscle failure, my son Aidan and I woke up early on the first morning of our new exercise program. Taking the literature seriously, I engaged quite vigorously in an upper-body workout. I'm happy to say that I hit the failure point several times with a couple of different muscle groups. At the end of the forty-five-minute session, I was completely spent. I headed off to the shower, knuckles dragging on the floor as I went. In the shower, I felt a sense of accomplishment—even peace—as I prepared for the rest of my day. And throughout the day, I had a glow about me, the quiet (and only slightly smug) inner satisfaction of someone who has woken up before the sun to make time for the hard work of self-improvement. The not-unpleasant "rubbery" feeling in my upper body served as an ever-present reminder of my early-morning virtue.

It wasn't until the following morning—waking up early again—that the glow was entirely extinguished. I was in pain. Real pain. Aidan and I limped through the short cardio workout prescribed by the plan, relieved that it took only half the time of the previous morning's weight training, and I hit the shower. I didn't understand just how much trouble I was in until I tried to wash my hair. While they were certainly sore, my arms still seemed functional while they were hanging by my sides. But as I reached up to apply shampoo to the top of my head, the muscles in my arms screamed in protest. I found my hands would only reach up as far as my ears. My arms were so wrecked, I couldn't touch the top of my head. I somehow managed to get through my personal grooming regimen that morning and headed into my day.

Throughout the day, I remember contemplating the possibility of quitting the program. It was costly in terms of time, it was *painful*, and even though it was still early, the fact that I had yet to see any results was frustrating. Yet due in large part to my son's enthusiasm, I found the resolve to stick with the program for a full week—at least until the upper-body portion came around again. I was curious to see if it would feel any better the second time. It did. I found that the exercises felt much more familiar and natural. And while I was sore again the next day, I noted with pleasure that my recovery was just a little bit faster and easier. There is little doubt that the magnitude of my discomfort at the beginning stages of the program was in direct proportion to my degree of lethargy before beginning. In other words, the amount of pain and soreness I experienced in exercising was a direct result of how far out of shape I had become.

The rigors required by the battle for justice in the world can come as a shock to the soul. Those of us accustomed to a more sedentary lifestyle will, no doubt, experience discomfort as we approach failure points. By definition and design, there is always risk associated with approaching a failure point of faith. The inevitable discomfort may even cause us to contemplate quitting the program. My purpose in this chapter is to provide a modest set of tools that will mitigate unnecessary risk while creating the kind of environment that can maximize growth. There are entire volumes written on these disciplines, and indeed much more could be written here.

The basic principle is that spiritual disciplines like those listed in this chapter have their most profound effect on us when practiced in the context of a meaningful and challenging mission. If we find little life or joy in the disciplines we practice, we should take a serious look at the mission we are on. On the other hand, meaningful and challenging mission becomes unsafe and unsustainable without a core set of healthy spiritual disciplines to undergird it. If we are experiencing burnout, breakdown, besetting distraction, or debilitating fear, perhaps we should take a serious look at the spiritual disciplines we are practicing.

Principles for Recovering Well from Failure

If the idea of the failure point of faith resonates with you, then perhaps it is because you have experienced it. Perhaps you have found yourself in a situation where the faith you brought with you simply failed in the face of the challenge you are confronting. If you can recall such a time, spend a few minutes reflecting on what you were thinking and how you were feeling. In most cases, failure points involve feelings of fear and anger, two emotions many of us find quite uncomfortable. We may find ourselves angry that God has not acted in the way we expected him to act. We may think that we have significantly misunderstood the character and nature of God. This may, in part, be true.

As important as it is to process these thoughts and feelings, there are two key things to remember. The first is that God has not changed simply because our experience of the world and our experience of our faith seem to have changed in a challenging circumstance. Second, it is important that our faith be tested. In fact, if it remains *un*tested, how will we know it is faith? Faith and love are quite similar in this way. Love proves itself most profoundly in adversity. It is when our love for our spouses, parents, children, or friends is tested by disagreement, disobedience, or bad choices that its mettle is proven. But the feelings resulting from our faith or our love being tested can be painful and powerful. Sometimes the hurt and confusion are strong enough that we are tempted to drastically rework the tenets of our faith—or to give up the program entirely.

Obviously, quitting the program entirely is a mistake, but how is it to be avoided? If the failure point is to be seen as a positive, faith-building place, how do we approach it with the level of caution and respect it deserves? How do we ensure that we will recover stronger and ready for the next challenge? How do we decrease the soreness and recovery time for the next failure point experience?

At IJM, our frontline investigators, lawyers, and aftercare teams are confronted with the kind of realities that can push them to the failure point every day, and even the staff who are more physically removed from this work are brought close through our daily practice of intercession. So on any given day, any member of our team can hear a casework update that pushes them toward the failure point. This is why a set of corporate spiritual disciplines are so valuable for us at IJM—to make sure that as we approach the failure point, over and over, we are equipped to recover from it. As you contemplate engaging in the work of justice, I would encourage you to think carefully about how you will recover from the failure point—before you hit it. The following suggestions should get you started.

Never Work Out Alone

It's surprising how often this simple rule is violated. Perhaps this is because the church in North America, as in much of the developed world, has become individualized. We tend to relate to God as individual entities, even in our corporate worship settings. Historically, this individualized version of faith is quite a new development. For most of Christian history the church has identified itself as a corporate body, a *we*. Today, particularly in the United States, we tend to think of ourselves primarily as *me*s in relationship with God. However often we spend time with other followers of Jesus, our own journey remains just that—our own. Our primary way of relating to God is as individuals.

I think part of the challenge lies in the limits of the English language. English is one of a few languages with a weak set of pronouns. The one pronoun *you*, for example, serves double duty as both singular and plural. There are some informal ways around this limitation (particularly if y'all grew up in the southern United States), but by and large it is left up to the reader or the listener to decide if the *you* in a given sentence refers to an individual or a group. By contrast, those who speak (or have studied) Spanish or French know that these languages have two sets of second-person pronouns, one for individuals and another for groups. In these languages, it is far easier to be precise as to whether one is referring to an individual or a group.

This may seem a small distinction, but consider the following passages from Scripture. As you read, ask yourself whether the author intends the *you* in each sentence to refer to an individual reader or to a group of readers:

- Surely I know the plans I have for you, says the LORD, plans for your welfare and not for harm, to give you a future with hope. (Jeremiah 29:11)
- You are the light of the world. A city built on a hill cannot be hid. (Matthew 5:14)
- Strive first for the kingdom of God and his righteousness,

and all these things will be given to you as well. (Matthew
6:33)
- Come to me, all you that are weary and are carrying
heavy burdens, and I will give you rest. (Matthew 11:28)

With each of these phrases, the pronoun *you* in English is rendering a plural pronoun from the original language. But without
knowing that, it can be almost impossible to tell. Why is this significant? There are several reasons. First, we need to appreciate that
the authors of the biblical material were more often than not referring to *a community* as they wrote. God's intention for us is that
we be interconnected, interdependent as we pursue him together.

We could make the observation that one of the things Paul
struggled with toward the end of his life was the difficulty of
isolation. In his letters from prison, he was constantly referring
to those who had been able to visit or those he hoped would visit
soon. In his earlier ministry, Paul had constantly traveled with
companions as he moved from city to city. He was not a solitary
figure but part of a band of believers, men and women on a journey together. So in a very real way, his letters (especially before his
arrest) are written from one community of believers to another.

Let's examine one brief passage of Paul's writing and ask our
"singular or plural" question:

> I appeal to you therefore, brothers and sisters, by the mercies
> of God, to present your bodies as a living sacrifice, holy and
> acceptable to God, which is your spiritual worship.
> **ROMANS 12:1**

Of course the *you* in this case is plural. But the surprising thing
here is that the words *sacrifice, living, holy,* and *acceptable* are all
singular. The plea Paul is making is that the many individual

believers in Rome offer their bodies as one single, united, holy, and living sacrifice. This corporate understanding of these passages has some bearing on the failure point of faith analogy: namely, that we should never approach a failure point alone.

We can take at least two cues from Paul. The first is simply that we need companions on the journey. We need friends and partners who travel with us, know us, support us, and require our support. The second cue is that we need "spotters" in the hard (and perhaps dangerous) places. When Jesus sent out his disciples armed only with a tunic and a staff (and some very good news) in Mark 6, he sent them two-by-two. The presence of a trusted friend can make all the difference in the hardest places.

During our weight training, there have been times—especially at the failure point—when I have needed help. I've gotten stuck under a weight I had partially lifted but could neither fully lift nor put down safely. In those cases, my ten-year-old son was an invaluable partner to keep me safe. He didn't have to be stronger than me to be a spotter. He just had to be there in case I needed a little help. In some very meaningful ways, the International Justice Mission family served as spotters for Blair when he hit the failure point at the magistrate's office in the middle of the rescue operation. We were able to pray—not only for the situation, but for him as well. Trusted friends were able to debrief the experience with him and help him sort it out. Similarly, during my experience of failure in Peru, my teammates were there to debrief, pray for, and support me.

All of this points to a simple truth: do not lift heavy weights without a spotter, and do not approach the failure point alone.

The Miracle of Rest

The fascinating and gratifying thing about weight training is that once you have worked hard at hitting the failure point, then your job is to rest. Rest is when the miraculous muscle growth (and repair) happens. In a regular program of strength conditioning, it is on the days off—the days you do *not* work a particular muscle group—that you experience the benefits of having done all the work.

Rest is also a prescribed rhythm of our faith. God calls his people to rest in the form of Sabbath. God even prescribed rest for the land every seventh year (the Sabbath year), when no crops were to be planted. This prescription to rest, however, is one we seem content to completely ignore. The Scriptures command Sabbath. Much has been written on it, and yet most of us avoid disciplined, regular rest. With so much to do in our fast-paced lives, it is perhaps understandable. But I'm convinced that the lack of rest in our lives exacts a heavy toll.[1]

To neglect rest in physical exercise is to invite injury and threaten the sustainability of the exercise program. To neglect rest in our life of faith is a far more serious matter. A significant part of my role with The River Church Community was to lead teams of church members on short-term trips to support ministry partners in the Two-Thirds World. While each trip was carefully planned against a set of goals conceived in collaboration with the ministry partner, we also designed each experience to lead (or sometimes push) our church members toward failure points. For some, it was simply coming in contact with the reality of abject poverty in the Two-Thirds World that led them to their failure points. For others, it was encountering a kind of hopelessness (due to chronic illness or lack of education) they had never before contemplated. The point is that a good short-term trip involves lots of failure points for as many of the team members as possible.

Over the years, we developed several strategies for helping people before, during, and after the failure point to ensure maximum growth and to minimize the possibility of negative effects from the experience. One simple strategy was *rest*. Each trip would begin with significant time and space for spiritual rest. This was sometimes difficult for participants, especially considering the dizzying flurry of activity that had been necessary to get them on the trip. There was the application recruitment, preparation, training, and orientation process. Then there was all the work associated with travel itself: packing, getting to the airport, making connections, landing in the host country, going through immigration and customs, taking in the first sights and smells, traveling to the place where we would be lodging, and finally, settling in for the first night's sleep. Then would come the dawn of the first day, the first expanse of time fully disconnected from to-do lists, cell phone calls, e-mail inboxes, housework, or any other oppressive, rest-stealing demand on our time. In this suspended state between the busy lives they left behind and the week of new experiences and work ahead, the first thing participants were required to do was *rest*. It is a lot harder than it sounds. Most people were itching to "get to work." They were eager to hear what the next steps in the journey would be. They were hungry to start contributing.

The idea that the first "job" they had to do was to find a quiet place to spend three hours alone in guided reflection came as a shock. While it was hard for some, we insisted that the team engage in this discipline of rest at the beginning of the trip. An even longer rest and reflection period was included at the end of each trip before the team left for home. What we found, almost universally, was that these times of rest brought order and meaning to the intense activity of the weeks spent serving and working. It was in these rest times that God seemed to speak most consistently, confirming and clarifying the work he had been doing during the much more active days of the trip.

Without these periods of rest, challenging experiences from

the trip would have remained unprocessed, the joys and triumphs of the experience would have gone unnoticed, and perhaps most important, many major lessons that had been packed into the weeks of service, observation, risk, and relationships would have gone unlearned. By refusing to rest, we run the risk of significantly restricting our growth, particularly after challenging experiences that have pushed us toward the failure points of our faith.

Cross-cultural trips are, of course, just one context where rest is important. As a disciple engaged in mission across the whole of your life, you must be careful to ensure that the discipline of rest is visible in various forms. Perhaps it might be helpful to assess your practice of rest. What Sabbath disciplines do you practice on a weekly basis? Do you have a discipline of rest that you engage in on a monthly basis, a morning or afternoon in the woods or at the beach? Is there some annual discipline of rest that you engage in, perhaps an entire day of solitude for reflection and rest? Just as physical rest makes your body stronger, spiritual rest is often the place where God not only restores, but actually strengthens you. To neglect regular spiritual rest is to risk missing the still, small voice of God offering to guide you in the journey—or worse, to risk injury as you push through the failure point.

A Healthy Diet

Any workout plan involves carefully monitoring what we put into our bodies. Because the nutrients in the food we eat are the building blocks of healthy tissues of all kinds, the challenge is twofold: we need to learn to limit our intake of foods that don't promote our health, and we need to maximize the amount of good, health-promoting foods we *do* eat. I think this serves as a helpful analogy for the development of our faith, particularly at times of great exertion, as we approach failure points.

One of the things I love to do is spend time with people

in the study of Scripture. I credit my years with InterVarsity Christian Fellowship, both as a student and later as a staff member, for instilling this deep love in me. I've spent countless joyful hours with groups of friends, students, church members, and my family reading, steeping in, discussing, and pondering Gospels, parables, psalms, epistles, wisdom literature, the prophetic literature—everything. The challenge with this sort of study, of course, is making it *practical*. It's important for us to learn the Scriptures and become familiar with the arc of their narrative, but what I find most miraculous and surprisingly joyful is the continual discovery that the truth of Scripture is remarkably relevant to my life.

When I began leading short-term teams to work in the context of partnerships in the Two-Thirds World, I always included this kind of Scripture study as part of the team experience. At first, I confess, I included time in Scripture simply out of a conviction that it was something we *should* do. But I soon realized there was something about the environment of a team working closely together, approaching failure points together, working hard and being stretched together that seemed to create a different kind of receptivity and openness to the Scriptures. This became evident from very early on. Spending two weeks together serving in a new culture and spending ourselves physically, emotionally, and spiritually, living in much closer community with one another quite simply seemed to give us a unique sort of hunger.

Time and time again I saw this play out. In the context of pushing ourselves toward failure points, we were simply hungrier for what God had to offer us from the Scriptures. It may seem trite to say it this way, but the living Word of God and the presence of the Holy Spirit were exactly what our tired spiritual muscles craved. Again and again, team members who in other contexts were quite unmotivated in their personal habits of

Scripture reading would report that they looked forward to our times together in the Scriptures.

Another way to say this is that vigorous exercise produces a different kind of hunger for a different kind of food than does a sedentary life. And eating good food after a period of intense activity is a much more satisfying experience! Our hunger for the presence of God in the experience of the living Word is perhaps most limited by how sedentary our lives become.

There is an adage among cyclists, particularly those who ride longer distances. They will often say, "Once you *feel* hungry, it's too late." What they mean is that during periods of extreme exertion, we need to learn to eat *before* we feel hungry. Hunger, physiologically speaking, is our brain's interpretation of several neurological and chemical signals. When our muscles lack the energy reserves to do what our nervous system requires of them, signals are sent to our brains that get interpreted as hunger, and we eat. So particularly during periods of rigorous exercise, if we rely on the feeling of hunger as our signal to eat, our muscles will already be in deficit. During sustained periods of rigorous exercise, if we want our muscles to be continually and properly fueled, we have to eat *before* we feel hungry.

It is interesting to note that waiting too long to eat during exercise has both physiological and psychological consequences for athletes. Waiting too long to eat can produce a state cyclists call "the bonk." When you are "bonking," you don't just lose physical strength; you actually lose the ability to make good decisions—often you can end up feeling like throwing in the towel, quitting the ride. This whole problem can be solved (or better yet, completely avoided) by eating a protein bar or a banana! The body gets what it needs, and the systems return to their normal state.

In some ways, hitting a failure point of faith can feel a little like bonking. What we *don't* want to do—precisely at this point—is deprive ourselves of the good nutrients we need in order to recover from the exertion of our faith. We should have a solid set of spiritual disciplines we engage in on a regular basis to ensure that we are getting all the nutrients we need—before we are "hungry." Especially in times of exertion, we need to be extra careful. At the times we are most deeply challenged in our faith, we should eat before we are hungry and drink before we are thirsty.

The "Along the Way" Disciplines

As I have journeyed with wiser and more mature friends into places where faith is challenged, I've been introduced to a set of disciplines that our spiritual ancestors developed as part of their own journeys. The set of practices that have become most meaningful to me over the last decade or so are those I've come to call the "along the way" disciplines. They are simple tools that help structure prayer, Scripture reading, and reflection so that I can more effectively notice and reflect on the transformational work God is doing in my life.[2] The simple beauty of the "along the way" disciplines is that they slow me down and encourage me to look more carefully for what I might otherwise miss: the still, small voice; the treasure in the field; the lily. One such "along the way" discipline is called the Examen.[3]

Ignacio López de Loyola was born in 1491 to a family of minor nobles in rural northern Spain. With few obvious career options, he trained for the military and became a knight. After being gravely injured in 1521, he had a profound spiritual experience during his convalescence. Showing the beginnings of what would become an extraordinary sensitivity to the voice of God, Ignacio López de Loyola left the military at the age of thirty to begin a decadelong pilgrimage that would lead him from Spain to

Jerusalem and then to Paris for higher education and ultimately priestly orders. At the ripe old age of forty (the very twilight of a sixteenth-century life), along with a small, diverse group of friends, Ignacio (known today as Ignatius) formed the Society of Jesus, or the Jesuits. These friends had all gathered around him while he was at university in Paris, each experiencing Ignatius's remarkable ability to guide others through a self-assessment process from which they would emerge "energized, focused, and able to articulate life goals and personal weaknesses."[4]

This self-assessment was something Ignatius called the Spiritual Exercises. The exercises became the central formational principles of the Jesuit order, a sort of "basic training" for Jesuits that lasted roughly two years. According to Ignatius, the most important of the Spiritual Exercises was one he called the Examen (or Examine of Conscience). In essence, the Examen is a simple process by which he encouraged his students to reflect over the last period of their lives (the last month, week, day, or even hour).

He would encourage them to find one *consolation* and one *desolation* during the given period. A consolation he described as a time, place, or incident in which the presence of God was particularly palpable, comforting, or consoling. And then he encouraged his students to reflect on a time when they had desired the presence of God, perhaps needed the presence of God in some discernible way, and yet were unable to sense it, and were thus left desolate. After some reflection, these experiences were shared with their companions as a way to process what God was doing in their midst "along the way."[5]

As an exercise, the Examen is deceptively simple. But for centuries, disciples have found it to be a rich and valuable discipline. There can be a tendency for consolations to correlate with "high points" and desolations with "low points." But with some careful reflection, we quickly learn that the consolation or presence of God can be experienced most profoundly at a desperately low place in life. And conversely, the desolation or inability to sense the presence of God can come at a time when things seem to be going well.

One of the things I think the Examen is particularly good for is helping us reflect on failure points of faith. In fact, it was during an Examen exercise that I first heard Blair tell the story of the challenging operation in South Asia. His feeling of not being able to pray, not being able to sense the presence of God in the crucial moment of the operation, was his desolation.

One of the first times I remember using this exercise was in Peru with a team from The River. Our friends at Paz y Esperanza had asked me to come to a support group for the parents of the survivors of sexual violence they were serving and (as a pastor who is also a parent) to give a talk to all the adults, offering them encouragement as they parented their children through healing from sexual abuse. When the request had been made, I broke out in a cold sweat but managed to say, "Sure, I can do that." I was forced to a place far beyond my own comfort—a place where I desperately would need God's help.

In a very real way, that experience contained both desolation and consolation for me. I was desolate and lonely in my fear that God would not show up—that I would fail utterly to bring anything of value or help to these parents who had suffered so profoundly because of the abuse of their children. My consolation was the experience of God actually showing up during the meeting. I had been thrust into a posture of trust I wish were more familiar to me than it is. And God met me there. Though I felt like I may not have been the most qualified speaker to deliver such an important message to that audience, I know from talking to the parents in the room afterward that it was important for me, as a North American pastor and a parent, to identify with them in their pain and offer what encouragement I could.

But the most profound consolation was the second half of the meeting. We broke up into groups to pray for one another. The parents shared their stories and asked for prayer. It wasn't long before all of us were in tears. The pain in the room was excruciating, but the presence of God was profound and sweet.

That night we debriefed the experience together through the lens of the Examen. I shared the desolation and consolation I had experienced at the meeting. As the rest of the team members shared their own desolations and consolations, there were more tears and a clear sense that we were at a very challenging place in our faith—but that God was *there*. The desolation was not the sense that God was nowhere to be found in the midst of the pain and suffering. The desolation was our inability to experience the ever-present God in the midst of pain and suffering. This very simple form of reflection helped us through the week as we sought to become more sensitive to the presence and work of God.

Growing in our willingness to reflect on and unpack the experience of faith failure is a significant avenue of growth. We choose *not* to reflect to our own peril. Unexamined pain and desolation are the breeding ground of resentment and can erode rather than grow faith. Rather than becoming more sensitive to the presence and work of God, we run the risk of becoming more callous. Unexamined joy and consolation, on the other hand, are a missed opportunity to experience the profound love of our Creator.

Questions to Consider

- How does your life include a discipline of community? Do you find yourself "working out alone"? What could be done to provide more meaningful relationships—people with whom you can be on the journey?

- What are your weekly, monthly, and annual disciplines of rest? How might you like to incorporate different restful disciplines into your life this year?
- As you take a look at the health of your spiritual diet, how would you assess it? What might it look like for you to "eat before you feel hungry" and "drink before you feel thirsty"? Is there anything you would like to change about your spiritual diet this year?
- What were your thoughts as you read about the Examen? In what ways might you incorporate this exercise as you travel with others "along the way"?

Snap here with your smartphone or visit the link to hear Jim address the three key things you need in order to recover from failure in a healthy way.

www.tyndal.es/JustChurch4

CHAPTER 5

The Secret of Joy

AMONG THE RANGE of human emotions, joy is one I particularly like. Like most people I know, I would like to feel joy as often as possible. But the feeling itself is one that is hard for me to describe. Certainly it has elements of happiness or contentment, but clearly these feelings are only a small part of it. Joy is an almost paradoxical combination of peace—a sense that at the most profound level, all is well—mixed with an excitement that makes me feel like erupting with a tremendous "whoooop!"

There have been times in my life when joy has seemed far off—even nonexistent. I went through one such dry spell as my wife, Jenna, and I were awaiting the birth of our second child. As our little family expanded, life was just crazy. All of my days were filled with ministry commitments, and I spent all other available time with a tool belt strapped around my waist, trying to make headway on building the house I mentioned earlier. I was exhausted most of the time from the combination of physical labor and lack of sleep. In the middle of it all, I remember feeling frustrated at the realization that my life was just not all that *fun*. So we set about trying to change that. Jenna and I tried to do a few things as the new baby's birth approached to inject some cheer into all the chaos, but the occasional dinner or movie or time with friends, while good, didn't really change the overall flavor of all-consuming busyness.

In the middle of all that frantic activity, Jenna went into labor. A woman in labor—especially your own wife—has a wonderful way of focusing your attention from many things down to the only thing that really matters! The days that followed, though perhaps even busier than the months leading up to the delivery, were a deep joy to me. I was there to "catch" Charlotte as she entered the world, to cuddle with her and with Jenna in the remarkable calm-after-the-storm that is the first few hours of a newborn's life.

The most profound experience of joy that I remember was during our first night home. We arrived home in the afternoon and visited with a few friends. Being quite tired, we all headed to bed early that night. At this point, we had managed to move into the as-yet-unfinished house we were building. We were all sleeping together in one of the finished bedrooms in the basement. Clara, then about two years old, slept in a small bed next to ours. And Charlotte, as Clara had, slept between Jenna and me.

Gradually, each of the three girls fell asleep, all exhausted from the huge changes of the last few days. Even as I write, a smile crosses my face as I remember lying awake for a couple of hours. I just lay there, listening to the gentle breathing of my wife, Jenna, my daughter Clara, and the infant Charlotte. For those hours I was flooded with the most overwhelming sense of joy I had ever experienced. I felt like the wealthiest, most privileged person on the planet. I was content, full, lacking nothing. And this feeling of joy had a sense of completeness to it, a sense of peace. But it was all I could do to lie there quietly. Part of me wanted to jump out of bed screaming about how happy I was.

My experience of joy, especially deep joy of the kind that God promises, is that it always comes as a surprise. I can't really plan for it, and if I chase after it, it always manages to elude me. Before Charlotte's birth, my meager attempts to season my busyness with fun activity yielded next to nothing. But God, in his creative goodness, was able to provide a kind of joy that was so deeply satisfying as to be almost intoxicating.

Having spent a lot of time in church—particularly evangelical churches—I have to wonder if we are confused about joy. It is undeniable that we spend inordinate amounts of energy in how we "do church" in order to elicit feelings. Services are carefully crafted to involve the whole person—soul, body, mind, and emotion. I think this is good, and I often deeply benefit from this careful work and pursuit of excellence. But I think there is a weak side to all this work that bears some thought.

The downside is that we can end up going to church week after week wondering why God doesn't seem to be showing up, wondering why he doesn't seem as present as he once was, wondering why it brings us little joy. So we try to season our experience of church by looking for new things to spice it up. We can add new worship music, go to a prayer conference, change the order of the service. But often the basic complaint is the same. Where is God? What has happened to the joy of our salvation? In an effort to solve our dilemma, there is a temptation to turn our focus entirely inward, pursuing just the right quality of worship or prayer to finally reach some sort of connection.

I often wonder how God views these efforts. There is a fascinating account of just such a standoff in the book of Isaiah. The people are angry at God for not showing up, for not responding to their fasting and worship. And God, for his part, is angry at the people because the form of their worship has become entirely detached from its intended function. What results is a sort of

dialogue that has become one of my favorite passages of Scripture
over the last decade or so:

> Shout out, do not hold back!
>> Lift up your voice like a trumpet!
> Announce to my people their rebellion,
>> to the house of Jacob their sins.
> Yet day after day they seek me
>> and delight to know my ways,
> as if they were a nation that practiced righteousness
>> and did not forsake the ordinance of their God;
> they ask of me righteous judgments,
>> they delight to draw near to God.
> "Why do we fast, but you do not see?
>> Why humble ourselves, but you do not notice?"
>
> ISAIAH 58:1-3

Clearly God is angry. Isaiah is instructed to deliver this message by shouting it at blaring-trumpet volume. But the problem
God describes is an interesting one. His people are seeking him
day after day in the Temple. There is some significant religious
structure to their seeking. This is somewhat reminiscent of Psalm
50:8: "Not for your sacrifices do I rebuke you; your burnt offerings are continually before me." But again, from God's perspective, there is some fundamental flaw, some essential disconnect
between the apparently correct *form* of worship that somehow
completely misses the intended *function*. God's tone is actually
sarcastic! "Day after day they seek me . . . *as if* they were a nation
that practiced righteousness and did not forsake the ordinance of
their God" (Isaiah 58:2, emphasis added). Clearly, God sees an
ironic disconnect between the people's perception of their pursuit
of him and the reality of it.

And for the people's part, you can hear the frustration in their voices in verse 3: "Why do we fast, but you do not see? Why humble ourselves, but you do not notice?" Aside from the second sentence being somewhat of an oxymoron (is it possible to humble yourself while hoping someone will notice your humility?), it seems the people are doing what they can to make a meaningful connection with God, yet he eludes them. Why is that? God goes on to answer quite clearly:

> Look, you serve your own interest on your fast day,
>   and oppress all your workers.
> Look, you fast only to quarrel and to fight
>   and to strike with a wicked fist.
> Such fasting as you do today
>   will not make your voice heard on high.
> Is such the fast that I choose,
>   a day to humble oneself?
> Is it to bow down the head like a bulrush,
>   and to lie in sackcloth and ashes?
> Will you call this a fast,
>   a day acceptable to the LORD?
>
> ISAIAH 58:3-5

God's answer comes clear and sharp. The people's "religion" is completely detached from the rest of their lives. Their worship and fasting—costly disciplines though these may be—are having no effect on how they conduct themselves in other spheres of life. Fasting simply as a private deprivation of food that causes us to wilt and mourn is not something that is of interest to God. If our goal is to have our "voice heard on high," it doesn't work. If our desire is the presence and blessing of God in our lives, this is not the way to get it.

What, exactly, is God indicting here? Is it the practice of fasting in general? Not at all. When we consider the Scriptures as a whole, we see God repeatedly call us to this practice. God isn't declaring the food fast irrelevant or worthless. God is calling out a much deeper problem—a detachment so profound that it would allow us to practice spiritual disciplines such as fasting in a way that has absolutely no transformational effect on the rest of our lives.

The word translated "righteousness" in Isaiah 58:2 is interesting. In Hebrew it is *tsedaqah* (pronounced tsed-aw-kaw),[1] and its meaning, rather than being simply "righteousness," is much closer to the combination of the English words *righteousness* and *justice*. This may seem like an unimportant detail, but because these two words (and concepts) in English are often so disconnected, this translation decision can significantly influence church doctrine and practice. Among other things, it makes it possible for us to think of Christianity as a disembodied spirituality that separates rightness with God from our social surroundings in general. It makes it seem possible to pursue personal holiness or right relationship with God and the benefits thereof (God's favor or blessing) while at the same time completely disregarding the injustice around us. But the fact that both concepts are included in this single word makes it clear: in God's view, we simply can't have holiness without justice.

So if these two concepts are so closely linked, biblically speaking, then why are they so easy, so natural, for us to separate? There is a long historical tendency for humans to divide life into two basic spheres: sacred and secular. In the sacred sphere, we try to contain all of our religious observance, all that we understand about God, and all that we do in life to worship and obey. The secular sphere, on the other hand, contains many of the unavoidable things in life: working, doing chores around the house, putting food on the table, changing diapers, or taking the car to the mechanic. While there may be some obvious overlap between the two sectors, we tend to see them as just that: two sectors.

Whether they are indeed separate spheres or whether this is an unhelpful, false division is an issue that has been argued at length by theologians and is not the subject of this book. What I will assert, however, is that if these two spheres are pulled far enough apart, what breeds in the middle ground is hypocrisy. In other words, if the sacred sphere of our lives becomes so far removed from the secular sphere that the first can no longer influence the second, we lose integrity as the people of God.

This is the very thing that has happened in Isaiah 58. God's people are crying out to him. They are longing for God. They are engaging in the structure of their religious observance and doing it with abandon ("day after day they seek me and delight to know my ways," verse 2). But somehow they have allowed this spiritual reality to become disconnected from the physical one around them. God is very aware that the workers in their midst are not being treated well—they are being oppressed. God is aware that disputes among the people are not being resolved fairly. But somehow, all of this escapes their notice. Somehow, as they enter the Temple, they are able to convince themselves that they cross some dividing line. They leave the secular and enter the sacred. They shake off all of the concerns of the world and simply pursue God—a God who, for some reason, remains elusive to them.

The deep irony they are missing (and that we sometimes miss) is that God *longs* to connect with them. He longs to pour out on them the very blessings for which they are pleading. But God's solution to their problem will be somewhat counterintuitive. In order for them to find God, they'll have to leave the Temple but bring the sacred with them back into the world (the secular). How will they find God? By engaging in the suffering of those around them:

Is not this the fast that I choose:
   to loose the bonds of injustice,
   to undo the thongs of the yoke,
to let the oppressed go free,
   and to break every yoke?
Is it not to share your bread with the hungry,
   and bring the homeless poor into your house;
when you see the naked, to cover them,
   and not to hide yourself from your own kin?
Then your light shall break forth like the dawn,
   and your healing shall spring up quickly;
your vindicator shall go before you,
   the glory of the LORD shall be your rear guard.
Then you shall call, and the LORD will answer;
   you shall cry for help, and he will say, Here I am.
ISAIAH 58:6-9

Perhaps the height of the irony does have to do with fasting. If I am so wrapped up in my pursuit of holiness, if my spiritual sphere is so completely separated from my secular sphere, then it might even be possible for me (with my abundance of food) to fast in a way that is entirely disconnected from the plight of hungry people around me. What God is saying is, if you're going to fast, for goodness' sake, at least have the wherewithal to share the bread you are *choosing* not to eat with those who have no bread at all! To do otherwise would be to engage in a spiritual discipline (with God) entirely disengaged from the other human beings around you. Fasting in this disconnected way could never be considered *tsedaqah*.

Jesus illustrates this very point with a familiar story recorded in Luke 16, the story of a man named Lazarus, who is starving and sick. He lives outside the home of a rich man—well, not the home, but the *gate*. The rich man has built an actual physical wall between his home and the outside world, insulating and protecting him from all the unpleasantness out in the street. Every day, the well-dressed rich man feasts sumptuously. Lazarus, his body covered with sores, longs even for the crumbs that fall from the rich man's table, but he gets nothing. The rich man pays him no notice—understandable, as he is probably distracted by his food and blinded by his wall.

Eventually both men die. Angels carry Lazarus off to be with Abraham. By contrast, the rich man is buried. The punch line of the story comes as we discover that the rich man—the one who seemed to have it all together—ends up in torment in Hades. Lazarus, on the other hand, is comforted in his experience after life.

We should be cautious what conclusions we draw from such a stark parable, but let us not be so overcautious that we draw no conclusions at all. The parable is a series of obvious contrasts and reversals. The first reversal has to do with the names of the characters. Jesus does not assign a name to the rich man. Everyone in town would have known his name, but for the purpose of the parable, Jesus doesn't give him one. The character who does get a name is the poor, starving, sickly beggar who would have drawn little attention at the gate of the rich man's house. Jesus names him *Lazarus* (or "God is my help"). In naming the characters this way, Jesus signals several other reversals that are coming.

Lazarus dies and is carried away by angels to be with Abraham. The rich man suffers a far less attractive fate. Again, this is a reversal that even Jesus' disciples would have had a hard time understanding. (I'm surprised they didn't interrupt!) Desperate for relief and stunned at the shocking turn of events that has landed *him* in Hades, the rich man calls out to Abraham for help—and as he does so, he addresses Abraham as "father." This identifies him as an Israelite, one of the children of God. And yet despite this religious pedigree, the barrier the rich man erected between himself and Lazarus in life—the gate—becomes a chasm that cannot be crossed in death. In life, it seemed that the character in trouble, the one who needed help, was Lazarus. In death, these roles are reversed. It becomes clear that the character who actually had the most to lose (or perhaps gain) was the rich man. His observance of his religion was so disconnected from the life around him that Lazarus was beneath his notice. Surely a child of Abraham like this rich man would have been aware of what had been written in the book of the prophet Isaiah. He would have been well aware—perhaps even able to recite—the injunction to share one's bread with the hungry. But the sturdy wall he'd built between himself and the world around him made this call easy to forget; it made Lazarus easy to ignore.

God's answer to this dilemma (the rich man's dilemma, the Israelites' dilemma in Isaiah 58, and our dilemma today) is intensely practical: bring the two spheres back together. Overlap them as much as you can. Tear down the walls that separate you from the world around you. God seems to say, "Engage in the world around you, and you will find me."

What's striking in this parable and God's words in Isaiah 58 is just how personal the commands are. God isn't suggesting that I should know the right places to refer hungry people so they can get food; he's telling *me* to feed them. He's telling me to clothe the naked, free the oppressed, and bring the homeless poor into my house. What might have changed for the rich man if he had obeyed? How might it have changed his own life?

> If you remove the yoke from among you,
>   the pointing of the finger, the speaking of evil,
> if you offer your food to the hungry
>   and satisfy the needs of the afflicted,

then your light shall rise in the darkness
    and your gloom be like the noonday.
The LORD will guide you continually,
    and satisfy your needs in parched places,
    and make your bones strong;
and you shall be like a watered garden,
    like a spring of water,
    whose waters never fail.
Your ancient ruins shall be rebuilt;
    you shall raise up the foundations of many generations;
you shall be called the repairer of the breach,
    the restorer of streets to live in.

If you refrain from trampling the sabbath,
    from pursuing your own interests on my holy day;
if you call the sabbath a delight
    and the holy day of the LORD honorable;
if you honor it, not going your own ways,
    serving your own interests, or pursuing your own affairs;
then you shall take delight in the LORD,
    and I will make you ride upon the heights of the earth;
I will feed you with the heritage of your ancestor Jacob,
    for the mouth of the LORD has spoken.

ISAIAH 58:9-14

What God promises as a result of obedience is almost overwhelming. Implied here is a level of connection to God, a level of joy that is hard to imagine. And in my repeated experience, it is a level of joy that cannot be achieved by direct pursuit. My experience in Peru proved again and again that engaging in the issues Isaiah calls out—injustice, oppression, abuse—is a surefire way to find the presence of God.

Another thing I find fascinating about both of these passages is the motivational appeal. Reflect for a minute on who stands to benefit more from God's people being obedient to his mandate. It's a hard question to answer. Certainly the oppressed who are set free will benefit greatly. Certainly Lazarus would have benefited greatly from the attentions of the rich man. But it seems like God wants to show us that the rich man in particular and the people of God in general have at least as much to gain: "Then you shall call, and the LORD will answer; you shall cry for help, and he will say, Here I am" (Isaiah 58:9).

Questions to Consider

- When you reflect on profound experiences of joy, what stories come to mind?
- Do you believe it is possible to achieve joy by pursuing it directly? Why or why not?
- Do you see any correlation between the situation described in Isaiah 58 and your own life? In your experience of church?
- What might it look like if the sacred and secular spheres of your life were more closely overlapped? Are you aware of what tends to drive the spheres apart? What does it look like when those spheres are too far apart?
- What do you think of the promises listed in Isaiah 58? Are they too good to be true? Have you experienced some of them? When?

Snap here with your smartphone or visit the link for insights from Jim on what God longs to give us—and what we're often prepared to settle for.

www.tyndal.es/JustChurch5

CHAPTER 6

From Mailbox Baseball
to Missional Risk

I HAVE A CONFESSION to make. When I was a young and wayward teen, I spent a few years wandering through a set of friendships that were less than constructive for me. These early high school years were turbulent in many ways. My family of origin was disintegrating. This left my siblings and me struggling to make our way in the world just a little too early. I realize now that some of my bad behavior during those years was simply a search for ways to vent the many frustrations I was feeling. But with little constructive influence, I was left to look for my own outlets. Some of the activities I chose were, to put it flatly, destructive. (I realize that my explanations of the causes of my behavior do not expunge me of guilt. Therefore, if you lived on a street called Albermarle Road in a small town in eastern Massachusetts in the late 1970s, please forgive me for what I am about to reveal.)

My wayward friends and I developed some interesting ways to while away the many leisurely hours we'd gained by ignoring our homework. One pastime we developed was a game we called "mailbox baseball." It involved my friend—I'll call him "Mike"—driving us down Albermarle Road very late at night. One of us would have his entire torso out the back window of the car, and he'd be holding a baseball bat. As we approached my neighbors' mailboxes, sitting as if on batting tees perched at the ideal height at the end of their driveways, he would take one swing with the bat at each mailbox. Points were awarded based on damage done.

Though it's been a few decades, as I remember this story (and several others), I still carry the familiar feeling of guilt—I knew this was wrong and destructive. But I've been thinking about just this sort of risk-taking behavior that is so common among young adults. My purpose here is not to get to the bottom of *why* we take risks; it is simply to point out that we do it—and with particular fervor during that time of life.

I have two simple observations to make about this behavior. First, the risks that are taken—at least those that come to light—are rarely constructive, much less heroic. They seldom involve young men or women taking risks to help someone or be self-sacrificial in some way. Selfless risks are the exception rather than the rule. That's why, when they happen, they often make the news. Second, it is easily observed that while most teenagers start with a fairly high tolerance for risk, that tolerance becomes much higher once they get together with other teenagers. In other words, while I was fully capable of making stupid choices on my own during this stage of life, it is astonishing how much stupider I was capable of becoming when I was with a group of people my own age. It could be said, therefore, that a "community" of teenagers exudes a perverse sort of "courage" that enables the group to take even greater risks than any individual would be comfortable taking on his or her own.

Several years ago I had a conversation with a colleague that also left me thinking about risk taking. She mentioned a nephew who had recently turned eighteen and was joining the military. This young man had grown up in a Christian family and during his middle-teen years had begun to struggle. His transition to adulthood was particularly challenging. As he and his parents discussed what would be best for him, joining the military seemed the most advantageous choice. There, his parents hoped, the structure and discipline of life would be helpful to their son as he struggled to find his footing in the adult world.

This is a time-honored choice. For generations—millennia, perhaps—young men and their families have made the same decision, often with very positive results. In this case, I was simply struck with the significant risk the family was taking on in making this decision. At the time we were having this conversation, the United States was engaged in two different wars in the Middle East. It was very possible that this young man's service to his country could cost him his life.

I left the conversation reflecting on this young man's predicament. There was obvious good for him in this choice, but as I thought about it, I was troubled by a different realization. Here, I thought, was a young man willing, literally, to give his life for a cause. He would certainly endure hardship as he was trained to fulfill a role in whatever unit he was assigned to. The training would be difficult but would offer structure and discipline. It would result in a whole new set of skills and capacities that would allow him to directly engage in a mission that mattered to him. The hoped-for ancillary benefit was some sense of grounding in the world of adults: that as a soldier, this young man would gain a new sense of identity that would become meaningful ballast in life.

Why, I thought, did the church have nothing quite comparable to offer young people ready to risk everything? Should not the church have a discernible mission that is at least as challenging, at least as compelling as the one with which this young man aligned himself? And what of the danger? When did engaging in the work of the church become so safe? When did it happen that living a life worthy of the gospel came to exclude the very real possibility of losing one's life? Should the church be living some sort of answer to these questions?

These are large-scale questions that are very hard to answer. But what is abundantly clear to me from my life in the community of believers is that over time, most of us develop aversion to risk of any kind. As we grow out of our teen years, safety and security become the predominant concerns that drive our decisions. Churches move out of dangerous neighborhoods, students are pulled out of public schools in favor of the more controlled environments of homeschools and Christian academies. We work hard to eliminate every possible risk from our lives. In and of themselves, these actions are all fine—I work very hard to ensure the safety and security of my own children. But the question does arise: How can we, who come from a culture that prioritizes safety and security perhaps above all else, become people willing to take the right kind of risks?

As we've already seen, the lives of the heroes that made up the first-century church were far from risk-free. The early church was in the habit of embracing risk and celebrating every time God rescued them from difficulty. In the last twenty years or so, I've begun to wonder if the absence of risk in the church is one significant reason we lose so many of our youth. Young men and women (like my colleague's nephew in particular) are far from risk averse. In fact, they are risk seekers.

What would it mean for the church to embrace this kind of risk taking? What would happen if churches actually began to *lead* in risk taking? I'm not talking about dumb, small-minded risks or pursuing danger for the sake of thrills. I'm talking about the biggest risk any follower of Christ can take, in any circumstance:

taking God at his Word and living as if it's true. This is just the sort of risk-taking spirit that engaging in the work of biblical justice requires of us. But how do we prepare? How do we ease ourselves out of our risk aversion?

You Get What You Measure For

A few years back we did an experiment at The River. We decided that for one year we would actually *measure* risk-taking behavior. We put some careful parameters around it, but essentially we encouraged groups of people to dream up some risk they could take together to embrace and embody the gospel in a new way—a "missional risk," if you will. We worked to remove any of the simple but effective barriers to healthy risk that we could think of. We led small groups through a brainstorming process to develop missional risk ideas. We offered financial grants from the church's budget for ideas that required funding, and we asked all small groups to dream up at least one risk they would take during the year. Then we tracked the results on a scorecard that we updated throughout the year, celebrating each risk as it was taken.

It was delightful to watch as each group went through the process. Some of the risks were quite simple. One small group made T-shirts printed with the question, "Need prayer?" They stood in public places and offered to pray for people. The experience, while risky, was extremely positive for both the small group and for the many people they prayed for. And I think it would be safe to say that none of the members would have been able to take this risk alone, but together this little community found their courage was naturally amplified. Together it was quite possible for them to take this leap, and it gave them something concrete to celebrate as their faith grew.

I remember working personally with another small group.

Because they weren't quite sure where to begin, we went through a brainstorming process in an effort to discover a risk they could take that would be aligned with their passions and skills. As a first step, we looked at the parable of the talents (we discussed the version in Matthew 25:14-30). Many commentators offer all kinds of different interpretations of this parable. We took a simple approach as we discussed it. In the Matthew version of the story, Jesus says that the three servants are given five, two, and one talents (sums of money) respectively, according to their abilities.

While many questions might arise about the differing abilities of the servants, there is one fact that should not be lost in the conversation: a talent is roughly equivalent to fifteen years' wages. Go ahead and do a quick mental calculation of what one talent would be worth to you. Two talents? Five talents? These are huge sums, especially when you consider that the people Jesus is talking to (and talking about) are largely living a subsistence existence. So the master gives the servants these huge sums and then goes away. The possessors of the five talents and two talents immediately go off and trade with them, eventually doubling their initial sums. The servant with the one talent lets his fear get the best of him, hides the talent in a safe place, and bides his time, waiting for the master to return.

The conclusion to this parable is fascinating, especially as we consider what behavior the master chooses to reward when he returns from his journey. The servants who have traded with their talents and doubled the initial sums are told, "Well done, good and faithful servant. You have been faithful over a little; I will set you over much. Enter into the joy of your master" (Matthew 25:23, ESV). It's worth pausing to reflect on the kind of risk these servants would have had to take in order to get such a high rate of return on their trading. I am no investor myself, but I do know that this kind of yield only comes at significant risk. In such high-risk trading, these servants were risking losing some of their master's fortune. And yet the master says, "Well done, good and faithful servant."

Then we turn to the poor servant who was afraid to take any risks at all with his one talent. Perhaps it's understandable from a certain perspective. Perhaps he's thinking, *These other guys could risk and lose up to* half *of what they've been given—and they'd still have as much or more than I have right now! I'm going to hide this one talent away and keep it safe.* But when the master returns, he is not pleased. "'You wicked and slothful servant!" he begins (Matthew 25:26, ESV). And it gets no better after that. Whatever the reason, the servant's inability to risk displeases the master greatly. And while there are questions this parable leaves unanswered—What if one of the servants took a risk and actually *lost* his talent(s)? What if he traded with them and didn't gain anything?—we can perhaps make several clear observations that help put things in perspective:

- The talents do not belong to the servants in the first place; they are entrusted to them by the master.
- The master seems to intend that the talents should be "in play" in some way rather than buried in the ground or kept safe.
- The master rewards a level of risk that in other contexts might seem extreme. (How much risk does it take to double any investment?)
- Sometimes we all feel like the one-talent servant. The assets and resources of others seem much more useful and worthwhile. *Sure*, we think, *if I had* that *many talents, of course I'd get in the game.*

Talking through these observations with the small group led to some clear and simple conclusions. It is quite clear that the things the master has given us are intended to be "put in play" in some meaningful way. And putting these things in play is going to require that we take some risks.

After our conversation about talents and risk, we brainstormed three lists of things specific to us as a small group. The first was a list of all the *passions* residing in the people in the room. There didn't need to be any specific connection between that passion and anything else. If someone in the group was passionate about it, it went on the list. It was fun to see people in the group calling out the passions they saw in others. Soon the list was quite long and contained things as diverse as "children's literature," "Internet technology," "soccer," and "the local Ethiopian community." The next list we brainstormed was a list of networks to which people in the group were connected. This list was fascinating and wide-ranging. It contained entries like "the teachers' union," "children's authors guild," and "church network connections." The final list was a list of assets the group possessed. We defined an asset as any material item, financial capability, or intellectual or professional ability that could be "put into play" for the sake of Kingdom mission. This list was also fascinating. It included extra cars, extra money, and spare rooms in homes. One husband and wife put their willingness to foster/adopt as an asset on the list.

The next week, when the small group met again, we reviewed our three lists and discussed briefly what surprised us in the lists we'd made and what connections we were making between the three categories of lists. At this point we divided the group into two smaller groups. Each group was given an hour to brainstorm potential "missional risk" projects and was tasked with presenting one or two of their best ideas to the whole group. They were encouraged to make creative presentations by use of easel pad and markers or whatever made the most sense.

I'm an idea person. I gain energy from open-ended systems where possibilities abound. I was looking forward to seeing what the groups would come up with. And when the groups presented, I was absolutely thrilled by some of the ideas. In scope, the ideas were *huge*. One of them involved using the children's author network to create a library in Addis Ababa, Ethiopia, to serve the community from which one of the couples had adopted several children. Another idea involved the small group coming around another couple as a concrete network of support (both emotional and financial), enabling them to achieve their dream of adopting children.

It was fascinating to think that all of these passions, abilities, and assets had been "buried" (so to speak) in the small group. But until we as a church decided to measure risk-taking behavior, we had no process by which to put them in play. The process we used was quite simple, and I'm sure more interesting and effective means could be developed. The point is that most of our small groups and churches have these sorts of resources lying dormant in them. What might be possible if we were to uncover and mobilize them? To be sure, putting all these assets in play requires risk. But as we've already discovered, if our congregations are to grow in faith, we must learn to risk together.

I've already mentioned the sad but inescapable truth that as we grow older and more mature, most of us become risk averse. If faith is a combination of belief and trust, then risk must continue to factor into our church experience. I strongly believe that churches that have learned to take risks and celebrate the successes that result (as well as the failures) are stronger and healthier communities, where faith is more than an idea. It is a discernible, living aspect of the atmosphere.

Over the last decade, International Justice Mission has worked with hundreds and hundreds of churches as they have taken the risk of stepping into justice ministry. Our church mobilization directors—many of whom are former pastors like me—delight in being in the room as ideas and possibilities are considered and plans are formulated. We're deeply committed to supporting churches in this process because we've seen time and time again that when we join the battle for justice, God provides us a pathway into appropriate risk and meaningful, productive trial. In the second half of this book, I will lay out a clear three-step strategy many churches have successfully used as they have started on the justice journey. It is a process that is adaptable to any congregation in any context, and it should be everything you need to get you going. The risks are significant and the trials arduous, but as James 1 so clearly says, in these things we can experience together the call of God into deeper discipleship and maturity. The needs are enormous and the tasks complex, but as Isaiah 58 says so clearly, engaging in biblical justice will usher us into the presence of God, where there is great joy.

Discovering Hidden Resources

At The River, as at many churches, we made frequent appeals for people to join ministry teams. Whether it was a children's ministry team, Sunday morning setup, a short-term mission team, or the team of small group leaders, we were always advertising opportunities for service and growth. Over time I became pretty confident that I knew all of the potential leaders who were part of the church. I learned just how wrong I was one morning soon after we began talking about biblical justice in our Sunday morning services.

The first time I shared with the whole church about our relationship with Paz y Esperanza in Peru was fascinating: I was amazed by just how many people surfaced in our church that we had no idea would be passionately interested in this new justice ministry. One of them was Mae, a marriage and family therapist who had been working for a county department of mental health. Her caseload was so large that she was constantly exhausted. Though she enjoyed worshiping at The River, she arrived late each week, and beyond the small group of friends she already knew, she had little energy to engage more deeply. Despite our consistent appeals for small group leaders and nursery workers, Mae had not yet gotten involved beyond her Sunday morning attendance. As soon as we talked about the survivors of sexual abuse we were supporting in Peru, however, she came forward. The consummate professional counselor, Mae knew the importance of addressing trauma in caring for survivors of sexual violence. She told me she would even be willing to go to Peru to provide any necessary training to the frontline psychologists working with these victims. In particular she said she would love to introduce the idea of art therapy and its use in dealing with sexual abuse trauma.

The capacity Mae was offering was exactly what Richard and his staff had asked us to find. While the counselors who work for Paz y Esperanza in Peru are well-trained and professional, there are aspects of trauma counseling that haven't yet made it into the curriculum and training programs for these nascent professions in the Two-Thirds World. Mae recruited a therapist friend, and soon we were back in Peru offering high-quality training not just to Paz y Esperanza's family of psychologists, but to the local judges, prosecutors, and police.

Sitting in those meetings, I once again had the feeling that an important shift was taking place. Hearing from experienced professionals about the need for quality trauma therapy significantly challenged the prevailing assumptions held by the officials who had attended this training. Long-standing practices of blaming and aggressively questioning victims without the assumption of innocence began to be dismantled. And at the end of the training, both Mae and her colleague were thanked wholeheartedly for the presentations they had offered. Further, some of the judges and lawyers who had attended asked if Mae would present to the local university and the local law school on these issues. She gladly agreed.

These meetings inspired a series of training sessions that Mae was invited to offer the following year with the goal of establishing a cadre of volunteer victim advocates. These advocates would accompany victims of violent crime from the time the crime was reported through the completion of the legal aspects of their cases. The advocates would understand the challenges victims were facing and would be trained to interface with law enforcement and prosecutors on the victims' behalf.

It wasn't long before Mae became interested in doing this kind of work full-time. In surfing the careers section of IJM's website one day, Mae noticed a position that seemed perfectly suited to her. IJM was opening a brand-new office in the city of Cebu, the Philippines. One of the key leadership positions needed in this new office was a director of aftercare. It turned out that Mae was the ideal candidate for the position: along with her considerable professional skills, Mae is Filipino and speaks three different Filipino dialects. While Mae's move to work with IJM full-time was a great blow to our little team from The River, we were delighted to send her off to this new opportunity.

Certainly for Mae, the decision to step out of her busy but stable life in California—even for a short-term trip—was a decision to embrace risk. She was comfortably established and had settled into her career. And on some level, she knew that putting her considerable talents into play in Peru might pull her outside her comfort zone. But rather than shy away, she embraced the risk and found great purpose and joy in the work. And she found herself hungry for more. The transition to IJM staff required even greater risk: an international move, the uncertainties of starting up a brand-new field office in a new environment, and learning to care for victims of commercial sexual exploitation.

Now, several years later, Mae is thriving. And her skills are making a tremendous impact on a team with a goal of actually *transforming* the community so that other vulnerable girls are never abused in the first place. Over the course of the first four years of operations, the IJM Cebu team partnered with local law enforcement to successfully rescue more than two hundred twenty victims of sex trafficking while bringing charges against more than a hundred suspected traffickers. But the really stunning fact is this: external researchers found that the number of minors available for exploitation in the commercial sex industry in her region plummeted 79 percent from their initial levels before Mae and her team began their work.[1] If you asked Mae, she would tell you that her decision to embrace risk has been a very good choice for her. But it's clear that it has also been very good for hundreds and perhaps thousands of other children in the Philippines who may never know who she is or what nightmare they have been spared because of her work.

Questions to Consider

- Spend some time reflecting on crazy risks you have taken in the past—perhaps in your younger days. What were they? What motivated you?
- Were there particular friends with whom you engaged in these risks? How did spending time with them make you more of a risk taker?
- Has your appetite for risk diminished as you have grown older? In what ways?

- What kinds of risks make you most uncomfortable when you contemplate them?
- What sort of "faith risks" or "missional risks" have you taken in the last few years? What motivated you? What feelings did you experience as you took these risks?
- Were there people with whom you took these risks? Would you have contemplated these risks alone?
- How does engaging in a risk with others make it feel different?

Snap here with your smartphone or visit the link to discover why engaging in more risk might be just what your church needs.

www.tyndal.es/JustChurch6

PART 2

The Justice Journey

CHAPTER 7

Finding Better Fuel

ONE OF THE PLEASURES of my job is answering phone calls from pastors and other church leaders who have been recently exposed to the work of IJM. People contact IJM for many reasons, but those who call my team—church mobilization—generally fall into three groups. One group is people who were previously unaware of issues of violent oppression and learned about them and the Christian community's response to them from an IJM speaker. The second group may be aware of the issues and may even be aware of IJM's response to them, but they have not yet determined a way to involve themselves or their churches. They are calling to learn how IJM operates in the fight against violent oppression and what it might look like to participate in some way. The third and decidedly smallest group is churches and church leaders calling because they are already forging their way into the battle against injustice and are looking for partnership, best practices, tools, encouragement, and help.

While I enjoy all three types of conversations, the most interesting come from the first and perhaps largest group. Every year,

my colleagues and I end up speaking to the staff and congregations at hundreds of churches all over the world. We deliver a
biblical message on God's call to the work of justice and illustrate it with hopeful stories of IJM's casework from around the
world. Invariably there are people sitting in these congregations for
whom this is their first exposure to these issues. For people who
were previously unaware of problems such as human trafficking
or modern slavery, the message frequently produces a mixture of
surprise, outrage, and impatience. The surprise and outrage have
to do with the scope and pervasiveness of the issues in combination with the deep and dark nature of the victims' suffering. The
impatience is about their sudden (and understandable) desire to
get involved *right away*—and to be directly involved in bringing an
end to the suffering to which they have been so recently exposed.
The early stages of exposure to these issues naturally lead to a kind
of excitement that is contagious but is not yet fully informed. So
periodically I will find myself answering a phone call that goes
something like this:

> Hi, I'm the youth pastor at X church, and I just heard
> an IJM speaker at another church in our town. I've
> spent the last three hours on your website, and I'm really
> thankful there's an organization like yours out there
> doing what you are doing!

Some conversation generally ensues about IJM's work and
how churches all over the world are engaging in justice ministry
both locally and internationally. Then the pastor will often say
something like:

> Hey, I was thinking, every year our church takes a
> bunch of kids to Mexico to build houses for poor

people. So I was wondering . . . how about this year we take some kids to Asia and free some slaves? Can you hook us up with a trip like that?[1]

Those familiar with the nature and complexity of this work know that it's just not that simple. While the church's desire to leap immediately into action is understandable, most often such leaps are impractical and unhelpful. This is perhaps difficult to read and may come as a frustration to you if a desire for immediate action is what you are predominantly feeling as you read this. But the difficult reality is that the work of justice is something for which most churches are unprepared. Church leaders are often surprised to learn that IJM employs hundreds of full-time professionals—the vast majority of whom are from the countries in which they serve. These professionals do this work in their home countries as both calling and career, and have invested in years of training in order to do it with a high degree of excellence. They want and need the partnership and the engagement of churches around the world—and desperately so. But the kind of engagement that actually serves the children and families who are suffering right now is often not what is pictured by a passionate leader anxious to get moving *immediately*. Before meaningful and lasting engagement can happen, there are significant deficits in education, vision, and exposure that must be corrected. Before the church can engage transformationally in the work of justice, it must itself be transformed. A foundation for the work of justice will need to be built so that our response to God's call can be deep and lasting.

The stark reality is that the outrage and impatience many of us feel upon our introduction to these issues does not prove lasting fuel for the justice journey. The good news is that *there is better fuel to be had.* There is a broader foundation to be laid.

There is a process by which the church can actually *build biblical justice into its ministry DNA.*

The church can and often does find very solid footing from which to grapple with issues of injustice both locally and internationally. And the truth is that the initial stages of outrage and impatience are part of the natural process. I see this every time I have the privilege of preaching at a church that is new to the work of IJM or to the Bible's call to justice. Between the simplicity and irrefutability of the biblical call and the compelling, hopeful nature of IJM's work with actual victims, there are many who are left with a sweaty-palmed, heart-palpitating "You don't understand; I need to do something *right now!*" sort of feeling. An early, headlong leap into action may satisfy the disquiet we feel in our souls regarding the suffering of victims of violent oppression, but what these victims *really* need is a church mobilized to engage for the long haul.

It may be helpful to reflect on the fact that those who perpetrate violent injustice upon the widows, orphans, and aliens of our world have not jumped haphazardly into their roles as slaveowners, pimps, and brothel keepers. They occupy their roles with a premeditated, focused, and sometimes deadly purposefulness.[2] And while these perpetrators of injustice may be aware that good people sometimes have strong reactions to the abuse of the vulnerable, abusers also know that people of good will often lack staying power. When we do show up, we have a tendency to arrive late and leave early.

For all of these reasons, it is only right to stop and consider carefully the cost of what we are about to pursue. Real engagement in the work of justice will exact a toll. It is painful, hard, and sometimes scary. Therefore, our preparation for engagement will need to be deliberate and thorough because the alternative is potentially disastrous. Without adequate preparation we not only risk running out of gas and giving up our justice journey without meeting any real needs, but we run some significant personal risk as well. Responding to violent oppression will lead into direct and often shocking confrontation with real evil and complex need. This confrontation often surfaces unspoken hurt, past trauma, and deep pain that has perhaps lain dormant and remained unaddressed in church life. A church or group that is not well prepared will often turn away at this point. As individuals face crushing personal struggles and approach the failure point unprepared, some groups will even feel "burned" by their attempt to pursue justice ministry.

I've seen this happen, and it always leaves me sad because when people turn away feeling burned, their losses are twofold. First, they give up on creating new ministry in their churches that could be potentially life-changing for those who would be served. Second, they lose the chance to have their own trauma and hurt deeply ministered to by a church transformed into a loving and safe place for victims and survivors of all kinds, including those who are already members.

On the other hand, if we enter well prepared, we will be ready to handle the costs and challenges as they arise. Our ministry will be more effective and more sustainable. Isn't a well-prepared, well-trained church just what the victims of injustice in our communities and around our world deserve?

Over the years, IJM's church mobilization team has coached many churches through this preparation process and into deep, real, and lasting engagement in the work of justice both in their own communities and around the world. The process requires a kind of patience and resolve that doesn't always come naturally to churches in the developed world. But from my experience, churches that apply themselves to a deliberate process of preparation most often find deep and lasting engagement that is transformational not just for the victims who are served, but also for the churches who are serving.

The remaining pages of this book will lead you through laying a solid biblical foundation and developing the necessary leadership, procedures, and best practices for justice ministry in your church. But before you proceed, let me issue a few caveats. It can be tempting to look at the following material as a *prescription*—a linear process for getting from point A to point B—or as an elixir to cure the pain in your heart that exposure to injustice can cause. But as you are likely already aware, almost nothing in church life is linear. There are simply no quick fixes to problems that require the deeper and longer work of transformation. This might be why Jesus so often used the life cycles of people, seasons, and crops to illustrate his teaching. And perhaps a similar metaphor would be welcome here. What I have attempted in the following pages is to identify the most important soil conditions under which the seeds of justice ministry can germinate and thrive.

It will be useful to think of this process in terms of a farming cycle. Producing the healthy fruit of justice ministry will require you to prepare the soil, to plant good seed, to water and tend it carefully, and then with watchful patience, to wait for the crop to mature. This rough outline and timeline might be useful to keep in mind as you walk your way through the phases of developing a justice ministry. In the real world of rain cycles, sun, and soil, the process of producing a healthy crop takes about a year. The work of developing a healthy justice ministry will take at least as long. My hope is that this will help you with the sense of urgency most of us feel.

The encouragement I offer you is this: developing a justice ministry is not easy, but it is worth it—worth it because God commands it. Worth it because of the many families and children who so desperately need rescue. Worth it because the ground in which justice ministry grows is fertile soil for discipleship. We are so convinced of the immeasurable value of a church mobilized into justice ministry that at IJM we have created *Dive*—a program designed to support your congregation as you discover how God has called you into the work of justice. (You can learn more at www.ijm.org.) *Dive* is structured around three distinct ministry phases: Encounter, Explore, and Engage. Though the work of justice looks different for every church, I've found that the three phases of Encounter, Explore, and Engage are essential parts of any journey. In the following chapters, we'll take these phases one at a time, outlining the activities that are most helpful in each stage and pointing to some excellent resources that have been developed to facilitate the process. I'll also share examples of real churches faithfully and courageously doing justice.

I strongly suggest that you read this book in its entirety before actually beginning the work of the individual phases. Gaining an overall vision for where the process is heading will be invaluable as you become involved in each phase.

One final word is in order. It might be easy to approach this part of the book as a to-do list, an outline of steps to take as you design justice ministry for your church. But if it is to be lasting, it has to be more than that. The coming chapters will take you through a process of engaging with the Scriptures, your church family, the surrounding community, and the world. The goal is to proceed with a heart that is as open and receptive to the Holy Spirit as possible. In all of your study, exploration, and investigation, what you are searching for are the moments of mingled fear and faith when you discover something—a need, a compelling opportunity, a crushing reality of abuse—where at the same time you sense the still, small voice of God inviting you to engage. While the process is different for every church, there seems to be something important about the presence of risk and even fear in the midst of it. If in this faithful place of discernment and discovery, if in this place of invitation from the God of justice you start to feel just a little bit afraid, perhaps you will know you are on the right track.

Questions to Consider

- Why is it important to slow down before getting involved in the work of justice? How do you react to this idea?
- As you think about the Encounter, Explore, and Engage phases, do you have the patience for a full growing season?
- Why do you think anger and outrage are short-lived fuel in the work of justice? What kinds of fuel would last longer?
- Recall a time when you sensed God calling you to do something (to initiate a difficult conversation, say yes or no to a certain opportunity, step out in some new way). What role did the feeling of fear play in that experience?

Snap here with your smartphone or visit the link to identify what's fueling your desire for biblical justice—and whether it's lasting fuel.

www.tyndal.es/JustChurch7

CHAPTER 8

Encounter: Meeting the God of Justice in an Unjust World

DURING MY YEARS as a pastor, I spent a lot of time thinking about the "diet" of teaching that my church—indeed, the majority of churches in the United States—regularly receives. As I've already mentioned, most churches are doing an excellent job of educating their congregants in the *belief* systems of the faith. This great work is aided by an overwhelming number of resources: new believer's classes, Bible study materials, multiple Bible translations and reading programs, computer materials, websites, blogs, popular books, scholarly works, and reference tools. The preponderance of the material these days is written and developed in English. There is an enormous English-language market because the evangelical churches of English-speaking countries like the United States are highly literate and represent some of the most highly educated, materially privileged people on the planet today.

During one of my trips to Peru, I had the opportunity to spend a day with a group of about eighty local pastors. Some were from rural settings, some from the city of Huánuco itself. Some of these colleagues had walked eight hours to attend this training cohosted by IJM and The River. Over the course of this day of training, I had a somewhat startling realization. I had known that one significant struggle for these pastors was the lack of educational resources, both for them as pastors and for their congregants as disciples. What knowledge and resources they did have they were eager to put to immediate use. It was a delight to see. My startling realization had to do with the fact that most of my friends back home at The River had a higher level of education than most of the pastors who attended the conference. It wasn't just that my friends in Silicon Valley had university and often advanced degrees; this aspect of the disparity had been clear to me from the beginning. The startling realization was that beyond all this formal education, many of them also had shelves full of Christian books on discipleship, Scripture study, theology, doctrine, pastoral counseling—covering virtually every aspect of the life of faith. The resources to which they all had access—and that many had actually read—meant that many of them were significantly more educated *as Christians* than the pastors attending our seminar.

As I pondered this realization, it produced several observations. The first was that the high level of education of congregants in North America ought to translate to a significant resource and responsibility ("to whom much has been given," Luke 12:48), and I'm not sure it really does. The second was that for all the sometimes-insipid generalizations that are made about "the great faith of the poor," I was deeply challenged by the faithfulness and commitment of the pastors who turned out for this simple day of training. What they *did* know had produced a level of action, response, and obedience that was convicting to me and easily outpaced their well-educated counterparts in North America. That is to say, there was a kind of *leanness* to the faith of these brothers and sisters that was inspiring.

As a person who enjoys learning and reading and who has access to an overwhelming flood of English-language Christian educational materials, I began to wonder if there was some aspect to my pursuit of knowledge that might be gluttonous. With the steady diet of rich teaching that was my experience in my North American context, was I running the risk of becoming spiritually obese and sedentary as I consumed more and more? In the language of a pastor friend, had I been educated beyond my level of obedience?

Here's the danger: with so many great educational resources available to us, we often see educating ourselves more and more as the "works" without which the apostle James declares our faith "dead." But I don't think God ever intended us to view the wonderful array of educational resources as anything beyond fuel to prepare us for action. Many of the pastors I met in Peru had never preached a sermon on justice, despite the heavy toll injustice had exacted on their neighbors and communities and the clear directive in Scripture to address it. You would think that given the steady stream of educational material available to the North American church, we wouldn't suffer from the same deficit. But we do—and the abundance of resources we have to illuminate the Scriptures should make this absence all the more conspicuous.

Why is it that sermons on biblical justice are so seldom preached—here, in Peru, or anywhere? Why is it that the glaring global justice issues of our day—issues such as sex trafficking, modern slavery, illegal property seizure, and sexual assault—are so seldom addressed in our churches? Why is it that the widows, orphans, aliens, and strangers so often mentioned in the Scriptures are so seldom mentioned (or present) in our churches?

The reasons, of course, are many. But I want to offer one perspective and one potential corrective. I think the solution actually begins with a different kind of education.

The Not-So-Merry-Go-Round

During the years I was on staff at The River Church Community, my family lived in downtown San Jose. My kids, especially when they were young, loved to visit playgrounds around the city. One that we frequented had a merry-go-round that my kids loved. It was a simple lazy Susan–type disk about twelve feet in diameter. The kids would gleefully climb on, and my job was to push them. Round and round they would go, yelling, "Faster!" One of the things they loved about the merry-go-round was the very real battle against the centrifugal force, which would push them toward the edge of the ride the faster it turned. They would squeal as they resisted this growing force. They would work against it and try to make their way to the middle of the merry-go-round. It was hard work, but they found there were bars and things on the disk they could use to work their way toward the center.

As they did this, two things would happen. First, moving toward the center would make the disk accelerate significantly, even though I had usually stopped pushing by this point. And second, if they were able to make it to the center of the disk, the force pushing them to the outside would suddenly become imperceptible. Making it to the center meant they could ride the merry-go-round without feeling the force. That didn't mean the force was gone; it just meant they could no longer feel it because of where they were located.

The downside, of course, was that sitting in the center for very long at all would cause them to feel queasy from all the spinning.[1] Inevitably they would get off the merry-go-round feeling sick and would stagger off to the swings or some other piece of playground equipment that would not make them want to vomit. Oddly enough, though, every time we returned to this playground, the first thing they wanted to do was ride the merry-go-round! Knowing it would do no good, I still felt compelled to remind them of what happened last time. I would warn them how they would feel when they got off the ride. And yet every time, they'd climb on. As I pushed them, they'd yell, "Faster! Faster!" They would move toward the center, accelerate, spin around, and feel queasy.

Over time I developed the growing sense that many churches in the United States were contending with a merry-go-round spiral of their own. Our world, the immediate reality we experience from day to day, is like the disk of the merry-go-round. Many of us are, to varying extents, aware that a larger world exists around us. And many of us know that this larger world is full of all manner of complexity and suffering. We may also be aware of some force compelling us toward the outer edge of our spinning world—toward the suffering of others—a centrifugal force encouraging us away from the center of our own little world.

But for so many of us, there are ample reasons to resist this force. Perhaps, having achieved some sense of security ourselves, we are thankful to remain separate from the instability and suffering that still exists for others in the larger world. Especially as we contemplate raising the next generation, maybe we discover a natural and understandable preference to be as far away from the larger world as we can get. Poverty in general and impoverished places in particular have risks and dangers associated with them. Many of us have been taught to move farther and farther away from that wider world and its attendant dangers. We've been encouraged to isolate and insulate ourselves by moving closer to the center—into suburbs and other "safe" communities.

So we spin, acted upon by two opposing forces. The God of the Scriptures issues his call to action on behalf of the wider world. The centrifugal call of the Scriptures is an outward force. It is an invitation to join God on his mission to a hurting world, to overlap as much as possible the sacred and secular spheres of our lives—to tear down the wall between us and Lazarus.

But like my kids—and too often like myself—our natural response is one of resistance rather than resignation to this force. We exert energy and effort to climb closer and closer to the center of our spinning worlds. And a strange thing happens. As we approach the center, the velocity increases. The effect of this acceleration makes it seem even more risky to move toward the outside. The dangers seem even more present, even more concerning. And we press on toward the center.

Should we actually arrive at the center, however, something unexpected awaits us: the effect of the centrifugal force becomes imperceptible. The effect of our inward journey is that finally we sit alone at the center of our spinning worlds feeling no compulsion to move at all. We lose touch with the reality of the wider world almost completely. And perhaps more alarmingly, we lose our sense of God's compelling call outward. We assume that the voice and mission of God (to the extent we can hear it at all) are limited to our own small, spinning world.

A Self-Reinforcing Spiral

I see the symptoms of this in churches all the time. I see it most profoundly when churches lose touch with two things. First, they lose the ability to see the world as it really is. It can happen to any of us, churches in the affluent suburbs as well as churches in the inner city. It can happen to churches north of the equator or south. Any of us can choose to live under the delusion that the only world that exists is the one we can see from where we sit or the one we see looking out the windows of our cars as we drive down the expressway. Our world becomes small.

Second, we lose the ability to hear the Scriptures in their

entirety. There are entire passages of the Bible left unread and unpreached from our pulpits. The passages that *are* read are interpreted as speaking to our limited world in a limited way, a message from God to our own individual hearts. So we are left in an accelerating spiral. We are unable to hear the Scriptures clearly because we cannot see the world clearly. We do not engage the world beyond ourselves because we do not hear the call to do so from the Scriptures. It is a self-reinforcing spiral, and the velocity increases until we finally reach the middle—where ultimately we become unable to perceive the call of God to move out and engage the world.

I made the fairly direct statement earlier that poverty in general and impoverished places in particular have risks and danger associated with them. I'm aware that this is a sociologically complex and perhaps even arguable assertion. It's not my desire to oversimplify this issue; this is just what I have found to be the case from my experience living in several different inner-city communities over the course of many years. Regardless of where we live and how we've been raised, many of us are well aware of the risks associated with poverty—with not having the safety net that a certain income, neighborhood, or family background can provide. We are also aware of the vulnerability associated with poverty in contrast to the relative security a more affluent life seems to offer. It could be this disparity that pushes us more deeply into our own, "safer" world. This is often why we move away from this perceived danger and toward the apparent safety of more suburban environments.

That being said, what many of us seem entirely unaware of, particularly if we've grown up far away from poverty, is that affluence also has risks and even dangers associated with it. In my experience, these dangers are real and every bit as perilous, but they are hidden in plain sight. Take a moment (without using a concordance or the Internet) to think through some biblical references to wealth. Which ones come to mind first? How many can you list? How many are positive? How many are negative? Are the strongest statements positive or negative?

While the Scriptures do speak of wealth as an evidence of God's blessing, it is also quite clear that wealth and affluence are among the world's most grave dangers, especially when considered from an eternal perspective. We would be guilty of a conspicuous (and indeed dangerous) kind of selective deafness if we ignored this fact. Below I've listed only a cursory summary of some of the scriptural dangers associated with wealth and affluence.

The pursuit of wealth is a never-ending, unsatisfying ordeal:

- The lover of money will not be satisfied with money; nor the lover of wealth, with gain. This also is vanity. (Ecclesiastes 5:10)

The pursuit of wealth can disqualify us from more important (and satisfying) forms of service:

- No slave can serve two masters; for a slave will either hate the one and love the other, or be devoted to the one and despise the other. You cannot serve God and wealth. (Luke 16:13; see also Matthew 6:24)
- Deacons likewise must be serious, not double-tongued, not indulging in much wine, not greedy for money. (1 Timothy 3:8)

Wealth acquired unjustly is a danger:

- Like the partridge hatching what it did not lay, so are all who amass wealth unjustly; in mid-life it will leave them, and at their end they will prove to be fools. (Jeremiah 17:11)

The allure of wealth can cause us to justify bad behavior:

- *See the story of the man whose great harvest inspires him to build bigger barns and then eat, drink, and be merry in Luke 12:13-21.*
- *See the story of Jesus throwing the money changers out of the Court of the Gentiles at the Temple in Jerusalem in John 2:14-16 or Mark 11:15-17.*
- Judas Iscariot, one of his disciples (the one who was about to betray him), said, "Why was this perfume not sold for three hundred denarii and the money given to the poor?" (John 12:4-5; see also Matthew 26:9; Mark 14:5).[2]
- *Read the story of Ananias and Sapphira, the couple who tell a completely unnecessary lie about the proceeds from the sale of their property, in Acts 5:1-11.*

The lure of wealth can hinder us from following Jesus:

- As for what was sown among thorns, this is the one who hears the word, but the cares of the world and the lure of wealth choke the word, and it yields nothing. (Matthew 13:22; see also Mark 4:18-19)
- Jesus, looking at him, loved him and said, "You lack one thing; go, sell what you own, and give the money to the poor, and you will have treasure in heaven; then come, follow me." When he heard this, he was shocked and went away grieving, for he had many possessions. (Mark 10:21-22; see also Matthew 19:21-22; Luke 18:22-23)
- Woe to you who are rich, for you have received your consolation. (Luke 6:24)
- The Pharisees, who were lovers of money, heard all this, and they ridiculed [Jesus]. (Luke 16:14)
- The love of money is a root of all kinds of evil, and in their eagerness to be rich some have wandered away

from the faith and pierced themselves with many pains.
(1 Timothy 6:10)

- Keep your lives free from the love of money, and be content with what you have; for [Jesus] has said, "I will never leave you or forsake you." (Hebrews 13:5)

True religion has nothing to do with the pursuit of wealth:

- Religion that is pure and undefiled before God, the Father, is this: to care for orphans and widows in their distress, and to keep oneself unstained by the world. (James 1:27)

This is a stark and challenging list. The implication is that as we move away from the apparent dangers of the world, as we recede from the dangers of poverty and economic instability, we run the risk of colliding headlong into the very real dangers of affluence. We run the risk of finding ourselves sitting alone in the center of our spinning world, no longer able to hear the call of God to engage the broader world around us.

But, you may be thinking, should this kind of isolation or insulation be labeled a danger—a soporific, perhaps, but a *danger*? Consider this: Once a community or culture finds itself affluent enough to insulate itself from the uncertainty of the world around it, it usually does. Once a culture has the structures in place to isolate itself from the pain and suffering of the world around it, it usually turns inward. Why wouldn't it? Healthy, mature people do not enjoy contemplating the suffering of others. And in the absence of a compelling reason to do so, we simply choose not to look. We occupy ourselves with the many other options to engage our time—ranging from meaningful and productive tasks to frivolous distractions. We are seldom, if ever, called to cast our gaze beyond the bubble in which we live.

The church never exists in a vacuum. External cultural forces always influence how individual churches and their members see themselves and how they read the Scriptures.[3] These things in turn influence the church's theological and philosophical foundation. Cultural isolation is a condition many churches in affluent areas find themselves in. In the living of "normal life," these churches and their congregants seldom come in contact with the biblical categories of poverty or injustice-related suffering.[4]

The absence of these issues begins to influence how these churches read, understand, and live the Scriptures. While there is no question that the Scriptures take the issues of poverty and injustice seriously, the question emerges as to how this concern must be interpreted. For a church living in such insulation, never exposed to the sin of injustice, the biblical call to engage the issue will be difficult to discern. A simple passage like Psalm 10:8-9 will begin to sound abstract or even irrelevant:

> They sit in ambush in the villages;
> in hiding places they murder the innocent.
>
> Their eyes stealthily watch for the helpless;
> they lurk in secret like a lion in its covert;
> they lurk that they may seize the poor;
> they seize the poor and drag them off in their net.

When I began reading the Scriptures at age eighteen, my life at a major university in the Northeast was utterly devoid of experiences that would have led me to believe there was a *literal* way to interpret this passage. I concluded, therefore, along with many of my friends, that there must be some more abstract, "spiritual" interpretation that made sense of this psalm—and of so many other passages in both Testaments. Having recently made a decision to follow Jesus, I was confronted by my own willful, stubborn, and repetitive sin. When I read passages like this one, I understood them to be talking metaphorically about sin crouching at the door waiting to drag me off in its net. (I confess that I didn't actually enjoy the Psalms very much in those days.) While this is certainly a true and biblical description of sin, I don't think it is a faithful interpretation of this passage.

It was a different kind of life experience that opened my eyes to a more sound interpretation of this psalm and so many more passages like it. At the end of my sophomore year of college, I spent the summer in Central America. While I had lived outside of the United States before, this was my first experience of life in the Two-Thirds World. I was directly exposed to a kind of poverty that I had, until then, been unable even to imagine. In particular, this experience opened my eyes to the dizzying gulf between rich and poor in much of the Two-Thirds World. But it was the utter *vulnerability* of the poor that left me reeling. I will never forget meeting a young widow in El Salvador. Not more than a year or two older than me, she had lost her husband to a terrible accident while she was pregnant with their first child. She had *no* safety net other than the church. The church became the literal home of this woman and her infant son. She cleaned and cared for the small building. And in turn, she and her baby were allowed to sleep there. For her part, this young woman was greatly relieved to have a safe place to lay her head in the midst of her grief.

I had read enough of the Bible to be familiar with multiple references to widows and orphans and the kind of care and attention they should receive, but I'd never seen it happen. I was dumbfounded by this woman's utter vulnerability, and I was humbled to be served a meal by her during my time at the church. Upon my return to my small world in the Northeast,

I found that this experience had left an indelible mark on me. And subsequent experiences have left no doubt that many of the Psalms (and many of David's in particular) are not abstractions: they are describing real life—the life lived by billions, indeed, the *majority* in our world today.

I relate this story to demonstrate just how effectively my environment influenced my reading of the Scriptures. Because my life lacked the experience of seeing those vulnerable enough to be mistreated in the way Psalm 10 describes, I simply assumed there must have been some other interpretation of the passage.

This fact—that our environment influences how clearly we see the Scriptures—is something we need to carefully consider. If the environment we live in is insulated from the harsher forms of suffering and need in the broader world, then our reading of the Scriptures will be limited. If our reading of the Scriptures is so limited, then what other compelling reason will we have to look outside the boundaries of our small environment to embrace the needs of the world around us? We end up in a self-reinforcing spiral much like the merry-go-round. In our pursuit of insulation and safety, we crawl toward the center. Our increasing distance from the world around us triggers an acceleration that causes us to work harder to reach the center, pushing all the while against God's centrifugal call to engage. But what we risk is the discovery that reaching the center of our own small spinning world will leave us deaf to the voice of God and feeling vaguely queasy.

The solution for us, counterintuitive though it may be, is to listen hard for the voice of God. And as we hear his call, we must find the courage to obey. We must work our way toward the outside of our small, spinning world. To our relief, what we will find is that each step, each risk, however tentative or small, will contribute to the slowing of the disk. Eventually, as we work our way to the very outside, the spinning slows to the point where we can safely get off altogether and see and serve the wider world around us.

Entering the battle for justice, then, will require at least two basic things of us. First, it will require a willingness to see the Scriptures as they really are: it will require of us the willingness to understand that God sees and cares deeply about the plight of the oppressed. Second, it will require our willingness to hear in our sacred texts the compelling call to move outside our small worlds and actually see and experience the world as it really is—inclusive of the suffering and pain that we could easily avoid noticing. In so doing, we will experience the invitation of God to engage the world at its point of need and to be transformed in the process.

An Encounter with Justice—for the Whole Church

Our goal in the Church Mobilization team at IJM is unapologetically ambitious. What we seek is nothing short of a spiritual awakening in the global body of Christ, igniting an unparalleled passion for biblical justice evidenced in the church's reputation for humble and courageous service to victims of violent injustice. There have been pockets of the church that have taken up this call through history, but our desire is to see the *whole* church— the global church—come alive and discover God's passion for justice and then take action. As you read this you may already be thinking of the people in your church or group who are most interested in issues of justice. (You may be reading this book because you are one of them!) But similarly, your goal must be ambitious—to bring the *whole* church into an encounter with the God of justice and the reality of injustice in our world

There are in many churches a group of "usual suspects" who, if a justice ministry formed, would be first in line to get involved. These responsive people are great resources to any church, but for several reasons it would be a mistake to hand the responsibility for justice ministry over to them and task them with creating and implementing such a ministry. While many of these folks will likely be central to the work that emerges, to sequester justice ministry to a small group within the church will inevitably limit its scope and impact both inside and outside the church. What we seek is the transformation of the *whole* church with respect to the call to biblical justice, not simply the development of a new ministry that would involve only some of the church's people.

Think of how your church approaches worship ministry or evangelistic outreach. Chances are that while there is a core team of appropriately gifted people who lead, develop, envision, and fuel such ministries within your church, it is also true that just about everyone in the church feels personally responsible as a disciple to engage in both worship and evangelism. Everyone may not feel that these areas lie within their primary gifting, but they most likely feel these areas lie within the scope of their role as disciples. Similarly, we need to understand that the core attributes of God (love, grace, forgiveness, righteousness, generosity, justice) should be reflected in our daily lives regardless of our specific gifting or passions.

As churches, we must approach justice (the attribute of God) and justice ministry (the activity in which we engage) in the same way. It is abundantly clear from the Scriptures that our God is a God of justice and that what is required of us as disciples is also clear: namely, that we do justice, love kindness, and walk humbly with our God (Micah 6:8). While each of us may not feel primarily gifted for the tasks involved in leading the ministry of justice, it ought to be part of our DNA as disciples to learn how to live justly and care for the widow, the orphan, the vulnerable, and the oppressed.

Churches effectively encounter the God of justice in lots of different ways,[5] but the most effective and complete strategies are multilayered and multigenerational. And while not all effective educational strategies begin in the pulpit, they will eventually include what is preached to the whole congregation.

I wrote earlier that we can sometimes engage in educating ourselves as an end in itself—a form of gluttony—consuming more and more resources, but not translating them into action on behalf of any of the real neighbors in our world. This warning remains true. But just as any trained athlete needs to eat the right food for the feats she will accomplish, your church will need to consume the right information in order to prepare for a healthy, strong justice ministry. So your Encounter phase will largely consist of building the right information "diet"—both from Scripture and from the world around you.

Justice in the Pulpit

Despite the recent surge in justice-related conversation around many of our churches, I'm still deeply surprised by how few congregations have ever heard a sermon on biblical justice. With a lack of solid biblical teaching on the subject and a plethora of voices talking about justice from a wide spectrum of perspectives, many Christians become uncomfortable when issues of justice first arise in church conversation. Not far under the surface of this discomfort lies a fear that these issues are neceessarily conflated with the realm of politics or partisanship.

Despite these initial concerns that may make us reluctant to discuss justice at all, the overwhelming truth from the Scriptures is that God calls his church to "seek justice, rescue the oppressed, defend the orphan, [and] plead for the widow" (Isaiah 1:17). There is no escaping this aspect of our call as disciples. So to those of us who are given the gift and responsibility of preaching, the articulation of God's passion for justice and the church's responsibility to reflect that passion is something we must grapple with and preach about. To be sure, there are churches and leaders who are bravely and faithfully carrying this torch, but the movement must grow because the passion for justice is a core aspect of the nature of God.

Take some time to review the last few years of teaching your church has received. If the list of sermons and topics has never, or not recently, included justice, it's time to consider it. If your church has had expository preaching on the Gospels and the Epistles and the subject of biblical justice has yet to come up, then perhaps now would be a good time to ask why. Or perhaps it's time to consider a more direct approach: an expository series on Amos or another minor prophet. Preaching on biblical justice should be as common as preaching on evangelism, worship, and tithing.

I frequently get calls and e-mails from pastors working through the challenge of preaching about justice. Generally, pastors appreciate help in two areas:

1. framing the concept of justice from a biblical perspective, and
2. defining what "injustice" actually means and illustrating what it looks like.

Obviously if pastors are unclear about these things, their congregations will be as well. I will treat each of these briefly below, including a few of the common pitfalls.[6]

Framing the Concept of Justice from a Biblical Perspective

You are likely aware of several passages or entire books of the Bible that might serve as excellent texts to communicate the Scriptures' call to justice. (You will also find a helpful list of justice-related

Scriptures in Appendix 2 at the back of this book.) But what is the basic biblical message with respect to justice that congregations need to hear? To what end does preaching on justice-related biblical material lead us? In short, we need to come under biblical conviction with respect to four simple truths:

1. God is deeply and passionately concerned for victims of violent oppression in our world. (Psalm 35:10; Jeremiah 22:16)
2. God hates this injustice and wants it to stop. (Psalm 10:17-18; Isaiah 61:8)
3. God's plan for ending injustice in the world is the church. (Matthew 5:14; 16:18; Luke 4:18-19)
4. It is actually possible for the church to engage injustice with efficacy. It's doable because God is with us and wants to work wondrously through us. (Ephesians 2:10; Philippians 4:13)

Addressing each of these four points will ensure that the resulting message (whether from the pulpit or in any other context) is balanced, biblical, and hopeful. You will also want to ensure that the message has a practical focus, calling the congregation to action (not merely to understanding). As you read on, you will find many tools and ideas for action. As you think about developing teaching on justice, strongly consider using the above as an outline.

Defining and Illustrating Injustice

It is far too easy to remain abstract in our discussion of injustice. Most of us walk around with some definition of the concept, but pushed to define "injustice," we would have a hard time being concise or concrete. Consider the following definition we have used at IJM:

Injustice is what happens when someone uses their power to take from someone else the good things God intended them to have: their life, their liberty, their dignity, or the fruit of their love or their labor.

Defining the term this way makes clear that from a biblical perspective, injustice is *sin*. It's not a vague or ambiguous category of things that just seem wrong or unfair or suboptimal. And it's not about people being victims of bad luck; it's about people being victims of other people. If I use what power I have to enslave other human beings or to steal their dignity by assaulting them sexually or to steal their children and traffic them into the commercial sex industry, I am committing the sin of injustice—the abuse of power.

A focused definition is a tremendous help in clarifying the issue, but a story makes the issue *real*. Hearing the story of Marta (pages 38–40) was my first personal encounter with injustice. It was an experience that enabled me to gain crystal clarity on the horrific reality of violent oppression. After hearing her story, I could no longer live in a world where injustice is an abstraction. As Christine Caine, founder of the abolitionist organization A21 and a passionate advocate for victims of oppression has said, "A million is a statistic until you meet one. Then they are a person." Sharing true stories turns statistics into *people*—people with names and faces. The abuse is real, and the effects are long-lasting. Clear, appropriately told stories have a helpful way of taking an abstract concept and bringing it into razor-sharp reality.

Some Pitfalls to Avoid

There are some very common and natural pitfalls we've become aware of over the years as we've preached and taught on biblical justice in a huge variety of different venues. Almost without exception, those new to teaching biblical justice are susceptible to at least a few of them. Here are suggestions for avoiding several of the most common:

- *Don't overdramatize the issue.* Those who are passionate about the issue of justice want others to be passionate as well. In our efforts to convince people of the horrors of injustice, we can be tempted to be unhelpfully dramatic. Issues of sex trafficking, modern slavery, and police abuse, for example, are dramatic enough without our overstressing or overelaborating. Doing so can often lead to people feeling overwhelmed and paralyzed rather than impassioned and mobilized. Most often what's needed is a clear articulation of the issue. You are not responsible to manufacture an emotional response in your listeners. You are responsible to tell the truth about injustice and the truth about how God feels about it.

- *Don't exaggerate statistics or stories.* The statistics and stories related to violent oppression are hard enough to believe without exaggeration. We need to carefully avoid any sort of credibility problem. The simple guidelines we follow at IJM may be helpful to state here: Before relating stories, carefully check all the facts. When sharing stories with others, give factual accounts without embellishing. (This was *exactly* what Richard from Paz y Esperanza did for me with Marta's story. Unembellished, her story was powerful enough to bring my faith to the failure point.) Be sure the statistics you are using are accurate and from a reputable source. It's hard enough to track reliable data about violent oppression, because these are frequently hidden crimes. Complicating this issue is that there's a lot of anecdotal "data" out there that can have a sensational feel—and no discernible research source—to it. If the statistics you are using fall within a range, either quote the whole range or just the lower end. (It can be tempting to quote the upper end only.) The UN and the US State Department have both cultivated helpful bodies of statistics and are often a strong place to start.

- *Give very clear next steps.* You have probably heard excellent preachers and teachers talk about the importance of calling people to action. Often the leading critique of developing sermonizers and homilists is that they lack a clear call to action (or "so what?") at the end of their message. When preaching on justice, this is absolutely crucial.

    Preaching on biblical justice, especially when done well, raises all kinds of feelings in those listening. Absent any clear next steps, hearers will often work hard to "pack away" the feelings and convictions the message raised. If we do this too many times, we can actually inoculate people against the message of justice. They begin to think, "Yes, yes, I've heard this all before, but there's nothing that can be done about it!" A few simple, practical next steps will provide opportunities for congregants to remain engaged in the issue and eventually become part of a growing justice ministry.

    If you lack clear next steps to offer your listeners, then wait! Don't *teach* on justice (especially from the pulpit) until you are ready to lead the church toward *doing* justice. You don't have to have the whole thing figured out, but you do have to have some clear next steps to offer—for example, joining the Justice Learning Community that I'll share about later in this chapter.

- *Provide lots and lots of hope.* The reality of violent oppression in the world today is crushing—not just for the victims, but for any of us who choose to compassionately contemplate the suffering of the vulnerable. When we teach about injustice, it can be far too easy to crush people with the stark reality of what we know. And after spending the time it will take to prepare a talk or sermon on the subject, you may be tempted to take people through the same emotional roller coaster that you had to ride during your prep. You will have to present the hard reality of injustice; that's the whole point. But you have to mix in very real hope so that your hearers are not overwhelmed with despair.

What we've found over the years is that the mixture of about nine parts hope to every one part dark reality is just about right. Where does the hope come from? It comes from at least two places. Hope emanates from the God of justice who hears the cries of the oppressed and effects their rescue. And hope comes from the very real stories of what happens when God's people show up in the lives of people like Marta. There *is* real hope of restoration for Marta. And as IJM, in partnership with churches and local authorities, continues to battle this kind of sexual violence against girls like her, there is real hope for other eleven-year-old girls in her community.

Equip Individuals and Small Groups for an Encounter with the God of Justice

While the pulpit is often the best place to begin, a continuing strategy to further educate individuals and small groups will be essential. Well-preached, the message of biblical justice is compelling. If it is appropriately combined with the reality of victims suffering violent oppression and the great joy of rescuing these victims, then the result can be both inspiring and convicting.

Churches do well to prepare in advance for this reaction. Having books available for those who wish to further educate themselves is an excellent idea. An even more effective strategy is launching a series of small group studies (perhaps six weeks long) on biblical justice, scheduled to begin immediately after the sermon or sermon series. This should be considered whether the church in question has regularly meeting small groups or not. It is a fairly simple thing to train leaders to facilitate these groups, and often a six-week curriculum is a relief to busy small group leaders who welcome the break from preparing their own curricula. IJM has many excellent resources to get you started, including books with study guides for small groups, prayer guides, and more.

Educate and Involve Youth and Children

Few will be surprised to discover that the issue of justice already exists as a passion among many of the younger generation today. Younger adults and students are often more aware of and connected to issues such as human trafficking and modern slavery than their parents. Those of us who have been involved in the justice movement for years have taken this as very positive evidence of the Holy Spirit's work within the church. There are many inspiring stories of churches who have actually been *led* by their children's or youth ministries into a new appreciation of God's passion for justice. While this is a very positive sign, there are one or two caveats that may be appropriate.

While passion for justice often exists among today's youth, it is not always accompanied by a theological foundation that grounds that passion to the bedrock truth of the character of God. My personal sense is that the onus for this problem lies not with these youth, but with their parents and pastors. Youth are responding to what they see in our increasingly globalized, media-rich world. They are many times more aware of and appropriately outraged by the savage abuses suffered by so many vulnerable people in our world. They have had a surface-level encounter with the reality of injustice—but often it has not been matched with an equally needed deep encounter with the God of justice. What they often do not understand is that the Ancient of Days has hated these same injustices throughout history and has built into his people the desire to respond.

I think that occasionally adult church leaders are intimidated by the passion they see in youth. The impatience with injustice that youth often express is sometimes dismissed as lacking theological grounding or gets labeled with pejoratives such as "slactivism," the sense that the "slacker" generation is angry about these issues but that aside from shooting off their mouths, they are not doing anything about it. To the extent that this is true at all, I think it is misplaced frustration and an unfair label. "Slactivism" is nothing more than outrage without an outlet. Because youth have not been appropriately led into action by the adult generation that preceded them, most of them (with notable exceptions) have very little idea how to take action themselves. I don't think it's any coincidence that my colleague Pranitha, whose story I shared in chapter 2, grew passionate enough to lead her county's movement against slavery after being raised by parents who provided medical care for the poor in their community.

The onus is therefore on church leadership to lead rather than label today's youth. Where else will the foot soldiers of the new abolition movement come from? Who will do the work of building a deep and lasting theological and educational foundation under these passionate people? Who will carefully guide them into careers that matter to God and to those suffering in this world? The job is ours, and it's time for us to take it seriously.

Taking this job seriously will mean at least two things. First, we must provide a steady stream of good educational and experiential tools to our youth and students. There are more and more of these available every day—IJM has produced several. (See Appendix 1 or www.ijm.org.) Second, we will do well to listen closely to the passion of our youth and carefully make appropriate room for their leadership in our congregations. As youth respond to what they are learning by holding fund-raisers and educational events, and later as they seek to engage issues of injustice locally and abroad, we need to make room for these initiatives. Doing so will offer an excellent opportunity for youth to take a prominent role in calling the congregation to the work of biblical justice. Imagine the positive effect of doing this exactly at a time when most youth are struggling for identity. This missional call to the work of justice can lay a solid foundation for lifelong discipleship and the pursuit of meaningful, Kingdom-relevant careers in the next generation.

There have been remarkable and inspiring stories of churches whose youth ministers have created brand-new material to ensure that their children's and youth ministries were infused with God's passion for justice. For example, Calvary Chapel of Delaware County, Pennsylvania, has done an outstanding job of educating their entire system of youth ministry. They focused first on the junior high–aged children several years ago, using curricula and tools to help them engage in the concept of biblical justice. As these students grew into their high school program, they continued their justice education. Now they have a whole generation of twelve- to twenty-two-year-olds who have fully incorporated justice into the DNA of their discipleship. By the time I received an invitation to speak at their weekend services, the youth were very excited—and far ahead of the rest of the congregation.

Deepen the Encounter: Form a Justice Learning Community

Once you've done the work of preaching about God's passion for justice; once you've offered the opportunity and provided the materials for individuals and small groups in the congregation to learn more about the scriptural call to justice and the reality of injustice-related suffering in the world; once you've provided some structure and direction to students and youth within your church, some interesting things begin to happen. More than likely, the wide net these initial encounters with justice have cast will catch people who desire deeper expertise in biblical justice. The role of leadership, then, will be to watch carefully as people respond to the movement of the Holy Spirit and begin to surface.

Usually a natural group will emerge as potential justice leaders. This group may contain some from the congregation who were passionate about justice before the Encounter phase began, but it will also include some wonderful surprises—people who didn't know this passion existed in them or people who have been passionate about justice for a long time but did not see the same passion reflected in the church. Some in the latter category will be people who have been sitting in the back rows of the church and have yet to become involved because they didn't see a place for their particular gifts, skills, or passions. A helpful next step, in conjunction with church leadership, is to carefully and prayerfully gather up some of these passionate, interested, and talented people who have surfaced through these initial Encounters and form a Justice Learning Community.

While the first steps of the Encounter phase have been general and broad, forming a Justice Learning Community (JLC) will enable a much deeper encounter with specific aspects of injustice.

A JLC is a multidisciplinary (and often multigenerational) group usually composed of church staff and volunteers who serve the church by taking the lead in further education and research on biblical justice. JLCs generally meet weekly (or perhaps biweekly) for a set amount of time (usually a few months) to lead the next phase of the Encounter process. In general the JLC will focus on at least three important things.

1. Continue Learning

Your initial foray into the study of biblical justice will reveal a wealth of information and resources on the subject. IJM's resources are a great place to begin, but they are the tip of a growing iceberg. A primary role of the Justice Learning Community will be to continue reading and evaluating everything they can find on the subject. Those selected to participate in the group will largely be self-propelled in this research because their interest has been piqued, they have selected themselves for this task (and been approved by church leadership), and they will have a role to play in the further education of the larger church.

It is an excellent idea to put someone in charge of directing and tracking the research of the group. This "lead researcher" can organize the work of the team and track the results of their reading and research by recording which issues resonate most profoundly with your church body and which resources seem most helpful for the stage you are at in your justice ministry development. You will find some excellent beginning places for this research in the lists of justice-related books, resources, and Scriptures that make up the appendixes at the end of this book.

A simple chart like the one following is a great beginning place for tracking the work of the team, but a gifted researcher will likely have his or her own way of tracking the work of the team.

Name of Resource	Evaluator	Date	General Comments
Book: *Just Courage* by Gary Haugen	Jim	10/2012	Short book written largely to frustrated Christians wondering if there isn't more out there, some "more challenging climb" that God is calling them to. Encouraging us to "get out of the visitor's center" and onto the mountain where God is at work. The call to justice is embedded through the entire book as well as several moving stories of IJM's work with individual victims and survivors.
Film: *At the End of Slavery*	Jim	10/2012	Short (30 min) documentary produced by IJM depicting several aspects of their work in Southeast Asia and India. There is a focus on the role of law enforcement (and rule of law in general) in the work of justice. This film seems appropriate for both Christian and non-Christian audiences.
List: justice-related Scriptures	Jim	11/2012	List provided in Appendix 2 of this book. A great beginning place to investigate what the Scriptures actually say on the subject of violent oppression.

2. Offer Continuing Justice Education and Discipleship Opportunities to the Broader Church

Not everyone in the church will have the same appetite for reading and research as the members of the Justice Learning Community. Nevertheless, it is important to maximize opportunities for deepened encounters with injustice and God's call throughout the entire congregation. This continued education is the second responsibility of the JLC. It is their job, in conjunction with church leadership, to prayerfully and strategically map out the remainder of the Encounter phase. Usually JLCs include church staff, but some are entirely volunteer led. In the latter case, the JLC can periodically report back to church leadership what they are learning as they develop a strategic plan for ongoing education. (You can find a helpful sample strategy for the Encounter phase in Appendix 3 on pages 249–251.)

This team will be well placed to evaluate the resources most appropriate to the church, and they will have creative ideas for

Potential Further Use of Resource
1. Use in a small group study. 2. Give to specific individuals in the congregation. 3. Encourage church leadership to read.
1. Screen for church leadership. 2. Screen for small group leaders (brainstorm uses of the film with them). 3. Encourage small groups to host living-room screenings in their neighborhood and invite their neighbors to come. 4. Host a large screening at the church in conjunction with a larger justice initiative (or as a stand-alone event).
1. Study one passage per week at JLC meetings. 2. Develop Scripture studies on some of them for small group leaders. 3. Host several Scripture "dig ins" on evenings or weekends when groups come to study this content.

how those resources can be put to use. They are tasked with thinking through all the different facets of the church's ministry and brainstorming strategic ideas to ensure the whole church encounters the reality of injustice and God's call to his people. Through the course of their own research, the JLC should also begin meeting with other leaders in the church for the purpose of collaboration. It is important to seek out all of the various church ministries in this process.

As discussions proceed with the various ministries of the church, members of the JLC can learn about what is already going on in these areas, offer various appropriate resources for use in that ministry area, and offer support for the use of those resources. The important thing is to develop a plan for the education of the broader church that will be both strategic and comprehensive. It is often true that some areas of the church will be more receptive than others. The JLC will want to begin where leaders and congregants are most receptive. And they will want to move forward prayerfully and with wisdom, building bridges between the JLC and the other ministries of the church.

3. Pray

The role of prayer is vital—indeed, we cannot meaningfully encounter the God of justice without it. The Justice Learning Community should develop a regular discipline of personal and corporate prayer as they begin meeting together. In prayer they will be continually reminded of several bedrock truths. First and foremost, they will consciously move into the presence of the God of justice, who cares far more about the issues they are researching than they ever will. Second, they will need wisdom as they research the various available books, resources, and tools. They will need to discern which are most appropriate for their church during this phase of their journey. Third, they will need help as they connect relationally with other ministries in their church. Invariably there will be roadblocks, resistance, and challenges. This is true simply because the church is made up of human beings, who are, after all, only human. The JLC will need God's guidance, patience, wisdom, love, and winsomeness as they proceed. They shouldn't hesitate to ask. Because these issues can be challenging to pray through, JLCs will often need to lead the way by offering specific prayer times and options to the church.

The Justice Gene

The goal of the Encounter phase is not a small one. If your task were simply to ignite outrage at the abuse of vulnerable victims of injustice around the world, it would be much easier. What you seek to do, however, is to engage in a process by which the Holy Spirit works biblical justice into the very discipleship DNA of your church. You seek to move through the initial stages of outrage and into a much deeper sense of conviction that the God you serve is indeed a God who hates injustice and wants it to stop—a God whose solution to injustice in the world is the church.

The ultimate goal of your Encounter phase is a church body that understands justice as part of God's call to his people and has some sense of what injustice looks like in the world today. In the chapters that follow, you will be developing specific ideas—discovering a new pathway into local justice ministry, new connections in global justice ministry, even ways to incorporate your church's heart for justice into your broader outreach work. But before you reach that point, you can begin by incorporating the behaviors and disciplines that are *universally* relevant to the work of biblical justice regardless of specifics or geography. In other words, disciplines like prayer and financial giving are vital to justice work in all its forms, regardless of where in the world the needs arise. Other forms of engagement will be either local (in that they address an issue in your specific geography) or global (in that they address a specific issue in your global networks). Healthy justice ministry will involve all three types of engagement: universal, local, and global.

I know it can be tempting to view an Encounter phase as something you have to "get through"—but I hope you don't see it that way. By taking the preceding pages seriously, you are seeking to lay the broadest possible foundation for what is to come: the work to Explore *(find real neighbors to love)* and then Engage in the ministry of justice. But without the proper foundation, it would be folly to proceed any further. The road ahead is fraught with challenge, complexity, and risk. As such, it is an ideal path for discipleship. But you need to be sure you are engaging this path as *disciples* rather than merely as concerned citizens or adventurous do-gooders. May you have the privilege of partnering with God's work to become transformed into the people he created you to be: disciples who do justice, love kindness, and walk humbly with God (Micah 6:8).

Questions to Consider

- How have you experienced the disparity of Christian educational resources between the Two-Thirds World and other, more affluent areas?
- Can you identify with the merry-go-round analogy? How have you experienced it in your life and discipleship?
- Are you aware of how your own context and life experience affect what you read and see in the Scriptures? How might you address this?
- Consider making two lists. First, list all the risks you can think of that are associated with poverty. Second, list all the risks you can think of that are associated with affluence. What do you think about these lists? Are you surprised by anything you see on either list? How might you work to address some of the risks to which you are vulnerable?

Snap here with your smartphone or visit the link to learn what mysterious thing happens when you and your church become aware of injustice.

www.tyndal.es/JustChurch8

Explore: Discovering the Intersection of Talent, Need, and Call

IF YOU ARE READING through this book for the first time, read on; as I mentioned before, it's best to get a full picture of the journey before taking too many steps down the road. But if you come to this chapter having just completed the hard work of bringing your entire church into an encounter with the reality of injustice and the call of the God of justice, allow me to congratulate you. You are among a small but growing group of churches and Christians who are beginning to grasp God's passion for justice, who view biblical justice as part of the DNA of a disciple. This growing cadre of churches who are coming to understand the dark nature of injustice-related suffering in the world today—and who are hearing from God a call to move toward rather than away from this kind of suffering—have become a vital encouragement to IJM and an essential support in the work of justice. It will be important for you to pause for a moment and celebrate this achievement. But it will be crucial for you not to pause for too long. In this phase, you will be exploring your own church and congregation, your surrounding community, your global opportunities, and God's specific call to you. As you prepare for this crucial process, you will find yourself at a challenging crossroads. It will be vital for you to choose carefully how you will proceed.

The Problem of Inertia

In my experience there are two tempting mistakes that are too often made at this juncture. If the Encounter phase has been well executed, your Justice Learning Community (and your church) will be angered, sickened, fascinated, horrified, inspired, and challenged by all they have learned. The emotional cargo the work of justice carries can cause many strong reactions. There are at least two that are somewhat problematic. But if you are aware of them, they become easy to spot and correct. Let me illustrate these reactions by analogy.

When I was young, I had an uncle who was an excellent swimmer and diver. At the pool, I would watch amazed as he performed dive after acrobatic dive off the one-meter spring-board. After noticing how transfixed I was by his display, my uncle asked if I would like to learn. I confessed that I desperately wanted to learn to do a front flip off the diving board, but that I was scared to try. To my delight, my uncle told me he could teach me.

At the poolside, he patiently explained the rudiments of movement that produce the necessary torque to achieve one complete revolution in the air and land feetfirst in the water. He talked me through the process several times. We even walked through it together poolside before I got on the diving board. He was a good teacher, and as I climbed onto the diving board,

I felt I had a good grasp of what would be required of me once I hooked my toes over the end of the springboard. But I found that standing on the end of the board and contemplating doing a flip was a very different thing from learning how to do it at the edge of the pool. I still understood the mechanics of the move—how to spring with my feet and direct my head downward and my hips upward, tucking my knees to my chest—but standing on the edge of the board and staring down at the water below, I found the move required more courage than I could muster.

I climbed off the board and stood with my uncle on the side of the pool. Again I asked him to explain the process to me. Again, patiently, he complied, walking me through all the steps in a clear and sequential explanation. Again I climbed up on the board. Again I froze. But this time my uncle called to me. "You can do this!" he encouraged. "You know everything you need to know. Just give it a try!" He sensed that I was tempted to climb back down and have the process explained just one more time, as if more education would make the next step of my process feel risk-free and devoid of fear.

He knew better than I did that there comes a time when you need to simply swallow hard and take the leap to put into practice everything you have learned. Making the conscious choice to move from belief to trust, I took a deep breath, swallowed hard, and leapt off the diving board. Following my uncle's directions, I found that my body executed one full rotation in the air, and I hit the water feetfirst, just as he'd said I would. I was elated, and as you might imagine, it was the first of many front flips I performed off the diving board that day.

I find that this momentary "freeze" on the end of the diving board is a common experience in life, especially when we are contemplating doing something new that is complicated or involves risk. And I see this reaction with some frequency as churches consider what it will look like to move from the Encounter to the Explore phase. The idea of making the Encounter phase concrete by actually exploring your surroundings may sound intriguing and even exciting. But as you begin to contemplate doing this, there can be a temporary paralysis that sets in. You may feel a strong temptation to climb off the diving board and seek more education, as if more education would somehow make the next step of the process risk-free and devoid of fear. But of course, there is no way to do this. There will always be risk.

For some, simply knowing this new information may begin to feel like enough. The last hundred years of church history—particularly in the United States—have placed so much emphasis on knowing what is right, that often knowing—especially knowing "more" or "better" than others—can feel like an end in itself. The great tragedy of this, of course, is that the hard-won momentum toward justice, carefully developed in the Encounter phase, will slowly dissipate. Over time, inertia takes over as the dominant force, and the Justice Learning Community never transitions into taking action.

You must exit the Encounter phase with a bias toward action. You must gather together the right people with the right gifts to move you into a very practical and clear exploration of the possibilities for engagement. Failing to make this transition to the Explore phase in a timely way can result in several significant risks:

- What you have learned may remain an abstraction. Without exploring the issues of injustice to which you are connected in your church, your community, and the world, all that you learned in the Encounter phase will continue to seem distant and slightly out of focus. The vital role of exploration in this process is that it begins to make concrete and specific the general things you learned in the Encounter phase.

- If you fail to engage your church in the exploration of your community and world, you may find that you lack the gifts you need for the ministry in which you desire to engage. So often it is the process of exploration itself that allows the church to envision and mobilize previously uninvolved members of the congregation with gifts specific and relevant to the work of justice. Simply put, if you don't explore well, you may never find those in your congregation who are most specifically and profoundly gifted for the work of justice.
- If you fail to explore carefully the issues in your surrounding community and in your networks, you will doubtless lack authenticity among those actually dealing with the issues in your community and world.
- If you fail to undertake the process of exploration—and undertake it prayerfully—you will likely miss God's call for you to engage specifically in an issue of injustice. It is in the process of exploration that you begin to hear the call of God to engage the issue in some specific and meaningful way.

Therefore, knowing what is true and right, while a vital first step, will never be sufficient. Your knowledge and beliefs must be put into action. This is true in terms of what you have learned about who God is and what God is passionate about. It is also true with respect to what you have learned about injustice-related suffering in the world. You must learn to take action and live in accordance with what is true and right.

The Problem of Momentum

While too much inertia seems like an obvious kind of problem, the opposite challenge can be just as difficult to deal with. It may be hard to imagine too much momentum as a problem, but as I learned by experience on the diving board, an excess of momentum can have painful results.

On the day I learned to flip off the diving board, I spent an hour or two mastering this new skill. But as I got better and better at it, the initial thrill of having conquered something difficult slowly wore off. I grew tired of doing front flips again and again and again. Later that afternoon, I approached my uncle. Flush with the pride of my accomplishment and satisfied with my progress as a diver, I was ready for a new challenge. "How about a backflip?" my uncle suggested. Still dripping water from the pool, I eagerly agreed.

My uncle walked me through the process at the water's edge. He showed me how to stand backward on the edge of the springboard with only the balls of my feet and my toes on the very tip of the board. He explained that this dive would require me to spring from this standing position, throwing my head back and my pelvis up while tucking my knees to my chest. The combination of these movements would give me enough rotation to complete one full flip in the air and land feetfirst in the water.

Unlike the front flip, this time I was eager. Having had enough of my uncle's patient education, I climbed up on the board feeling a few butterflies, but essentially confident that as an accomplished diver, I had the knowledge and skill necessary to tackle this new challenge. I carefully placed my toes in position at the end of the board with my back to the water. With no pause at all, I took a deep breath and sprang hard off the board, throwing my head back and my pelvis up. My body rotated around with ease—considerably more ease than I expected, as it turned out. I came out of my tuck in time to see my extending feet not enter the water as they should have, but rush by the surface of the water and rotate back up toward the diving board. Rather than the sound of my feet entering the water, my uncle and many others standing around the pool heard a loud and sickening *slap!* as I hit the water flat on my back.

I would later learn (once the pain and accompanying redness had begun to recede from the skin on my back) that I had committed the classic mistake of over-rotation. In a way, I'd entered the dive with too much confidence. My overconfident spring off the board had produced too much momentum. Rather than achieving one full rotation in the air, I had managed precisely one and a quarter rotations. It would take several days for my confidence to recover fully. And the next time I attempted a backflip, I was significantly less flippant (if you'll pardon the pun) about my own abilities as a diver. Clearly, too much momentum can be a problem.

As you may imagine, it tends to be different kinds of churches and leaders who struggle at the different ends of this inertia-momentum spectrum. Churches with a significant amount of ministry energy who see themselves as successful and trendsetting often have courage and confidence as they contemplate new opportunities for ministry. Such churches or teams may come out of the Encounter phase with a momentum problem. They may be so inspired and energized by what they have learned, they may feel so ready to sink their teeth into the issue that they feel too impatient for a robust Explore phase and instead try to leap straight into direct engagement. While this is understandable, it is problematic and can have devastating consequences:

- If you don't take the time for careful exploration and research in your community, others may experience you as prideful, knowing the "answers" without taking time to explore how others define the problems or the solutions that are currently being employed. (Beyond the problem of how others perceive you, this behavior may actually stem from an attitude of hubris that should be carefully examined.)
- If you don't take the time to build appropriate alliances with others working for justice, others may experience you as aloof, not interested in collaboration and partnership.
- If you don't do the work of building relationships, others may experience you as outsiders coming in to impose your solution on a problem you don't fully understand.
- If you don't honor those already hard at work, others may perceive you as dismissive of the labor of those who have been there longer and sacrificed more than you have.
- If you don't take the time to survey the landscape, you may unknowingly duplicate the efforts of others who are already at work in your community or the world.
- If you don't take the time to fully understand the issues and carefully design an appropriate ministry response, you may lack staying power.

As you read through this section, take some time to think carefully about the problems of inertia and momentum. On which end of this spectrum does your team or church likely fall? What would the consequences be for your team or church if you were to give in to too much inertia or momentum? How will you need to construct your Explore phase in order to account for this potential weakness? Will you need to set a careful Explore timeline in order to overcome some inertia? Or will you need to remind yourself to slow down and allow your team to fully realize the Explore phase before you take the leap to engagement?

Understanding the Goals of the Explore Phase

By way of review, the objectives of a successful Encounter phase are to bring the entire church into an encounter with the biblical call to the work of justice and the reality of injustice-related suffering in today's world, and to surface an initial group of people who are (or are becoming) passionate about biblical justice and who desire an even deeper encounter. But how do you know when it's time to move beyond this introduction of your minds and souls? How will you know when the Encounter phase should transition into an Explore phase?

The main indicator that you are ready to enter the Explore phase is a sense of biblical conviction about the work of justice. While you may have begun the Encounter with a sense of impatience, frustration, and even anger, you need to acknowledge that the visceral nature of these feelings makes them capricious. What will you do on the day you wake up and no longer feel an acute sense of outrage? Will you give up? What will you do when you encounter your first serious obstacle or your second seemingly insurmountable problem? What will you do when inevitable relational conflicts threaten the longevity of your new ministry? Will impatience, frustration, and anger carry you over such obstacles and through such times? Likely not. What will you do when engagement with real suffering in the world catapults your faith to the failure point? Will impatience, frustration, and anger facilitate a recovery in the care of your loving God? Almost certainly not.

The lasting motivation, the necessary energy to move inexorably forward over obstacles and through difficulty, must come from the source of all lasting motivation—from your Maker, who calls you to give up your life for the worthy cause of demonstrating (telling and showing) the very best of news to a deeply hurting world. So while you may not yet have a sense of what the church can or should do, if you have a growing sense of conviction that the God of the Scriptures calls you to do something, to engage in some way, then you are very much on the right track.

If a successful Encounter phase results in a church coming under biblical conviction regarding God's call to the work of justice, then a successful Explore phase is about finding real neighbors to love. All too often the concept of justice remains theoretical. Perhaps you remain content to stay in the Encounter phase too long, coming to an ever deeper understanding of the issues and theology of justice. Perhaps you become too comfortable in your role as the educator of others and settle too quickly into a moral conviction that others must know what you have now learned. But the call of the Scriptures is far too personal and practical for that. At some point, the Scriptures teach, you must actually engage with the victims of injustice. Like the Good Samaritan in Jesus' parable (Luke 10:25-37), you must be willing to cross the road and draw near to the suffering of your neighbors.

The goal of this whole justice journey is the mobilization of your church in search of real neighbors who desperately need the Good News brought to them. I have always been fascinated by Matthew 11:4-5, Jesus' answer to John's disciples who were sent to inquire if Jesus is actually the Messiah or if they should wait for someone else. John is in prison awaiting what will turn out to be his execution. Jesus, by way of answer, simply tells John's disciples to report to the prisoner what they hear and see.

And he recounts for them a long list of miracles—reminiscent of Jesus' description of his ministry in Luke 4:18-19—ending with, "and the poor have good news *brought to them*" (Matthew 11:5, emphasis added). It is in the Explore phase that you will seek to discover vulnerable neighbors who need good news brought to them.

Transitioning from Encounter to Explore

As you move into the Explore phase, the individual pathways for each church become more diverse and unique. But as with the Encounter phase, there are some general guidelines that will be helpful to follow. First, church leadership and the Justice Learning Community should carefully consider the people who have surfaced during the Encounter phase. Most often the people with the skills needed to lead the Explore phase will be those who surface during the Encounter phase.

The next step is to gather the leaders who have surfaced and commission them to lead the Explore phase. These leaders, usually a combination of gifted staff and laypeople, then form a Justice Task Force. (You can, of course, name this group whatever is most appropriate for your community.) They will be charged with the work of exploring your church, your community, and your global opportunities in a specific set of ways, outlined on page 152. It is important that these leaders be both passionate and mature. As they begin this work, the challenge they will most likely encounter is not a lack of opportunity for service and ministry. In fact, the most likely outcome of this process is that the team will discover an abundance of needs that appear as opportunities for ministry. And they will no doubt discover a wealth of talent in the church—some of it entirely new. Therefore, the work of the Justice Task Force will require careful discernment in the midst of many opportunities. The challenge will be to determine the best choice among many viable ministry options.

Becoming a Justice Task Force

Sometimes groups are tempted to let the transition between Encounter and Explore simply evolve over time. While this may seem like a good idea, there are several reasons to consider establishing a more clear distinction between the two phases:

- The tasks involved in the two phases are quite different. While the Explore phase will obviously involve a lot of learning, it is an essentially different task requiring a different skill set than the Encounter phase. It is often a good idea to mark the transition with the whole congregation, perhaps even announcing to the whole body that now that you have had this encounter with God's call to justice, the church will establish a specific team to explore exactly how the congregation, should engage in the work of justice.
- Those who led during the Encounter phase of the process are not necessarily those best equipped to lead the Explore phase. A clear transition between the Encounter and Explore phases will provide time for any natural leadership transition, should that be necessary.
- Once people have learned about the extent of suffering in today's world caused by violent oppression, they are often overwhelmed and immobilized. A period of exploration into specific aspects of injustice can have the effect of reducing the huge problem to a more manageable size as you consider becoming involved in a specific aspect of the work.

- Keeping the wider church regularly updated on the work of the Justice Task Force will help the congregation understand that the work is moving forward and will perhaps continue to reveal expertise and passion in the church.
- Finally, there will be a lot of exploring to do. We've broken this phase up into three distinct tasks—exploring your church, your community, and your global opportunities—which can be undertaken sequentially or simultaneously, depending on the capacity of your Justice Task Force.

Getting Specific

Following are specific steps for conducting an effective Explore phase. As mentioned previously, I suggest you read through this entire set of instructions before beginning the work with your Justice Task Force. As you read, you will discover that there are really two distinct tasks associated with the Explore phase: research and discernment. In some ways, the research portion is quite simple. You will be directed through a process of exploring your church, your community, and your global opportunities. As you conduct your research, you will seek answers to specific questions and report on what you find. The challenge comes in the need for discernment. As I mentioned above, your research will no doubt uncover various new people, talents, and abilities in your church. These people and abilities will likely align with several opportunities for ministry and service that you discover in your community and in the broader world. The difficulty comes in discerning the appropriate next steps, given all this new information. An essential part of this process will be remaining connected to God's passionate heart for justice in the midst of all this research. Perhaps the chart on the following page will help clarify the specific tasks of research and discernment in several categories.

Explore (research)	Discern
Your Church	As you uncover new information about your church, you are working prayerfully to discern the unique abilities your church has—the church's collective talents. (See the discussion of the parable of the talents on pages 88–89.)
Your Community	As you uncover new information about your community, you are working prayerfully to discern: • Clear places you can expand from evangelism and mercy ministry to begin including justice ministry as well • Clear places of potential partnership—where others are already effectively at work and your church's skills, talents, and resources might support or enhance that work • A clearly defined unmet need in your community that has some resonance with the people and talents you have uncovered in your own church
Your Global Opportunities	As you uncover new information about the places in the world where you are already connected and invested, you are working prayerfully to discern: • Clear places of potential partnership—where others are already effectively at work and your church's skills, talents, and resources might support or enhance that work • A clearly defined unmet need in your global networks that has some resonance with the people and talents you have uncovered in your own church

As you engage in this learning and discernment process, you must do so with as much sensitivity to God's Spirit as you can muster. This process is designed to surface as much ability and need as you can find. You will doubtless discover many opportunities for service, many possibilities for engagement—in fact, it may feel like *too* many. For teams beginning this process, every new discovery will seem to imply a call from God to engage immediately. You must be disciplined to discern the voice of God in the midst of it all. This process is deliberately designed to surface as many talents in the church as possible. It is designed to help the church uncover a world of unmet need in the surrounding community and around the globe. If you jump at every new discovery, your new ministry will be scattered and ineffective. If you try to meet every need, you will end up serving no one well. So how do you discern when and how you take action in order to invest your talent most deeply? You do this by looking for a clear sense of the convergence of three things: need, talent, and call.

Perhaps this diagram will help:

Three Key Areas of Exploration

Unique talent: What unique talents exist in your church body? What can you do well that might serve others in need? What people among you represent significant assets in your developing justice ministry? What resources can you bring to bear on the issues around you?

Clearly defined need: What clearly defined justice needs exist in your neighborhood, your city, and the worldwide networks of which you are a part? What can you do to discover specific unmet needs in any or all of these places?

Call from God: Where do you sense God urging or inviting you to engage? What specific problem or justice-related issue seems to ignite a passion that God is affirming? Where do you sense the mingled feelings of excitement and fear?

This graphic may seem like an oversimplification, but consider this: most churches possess an abundance of all three of these things—talent, awareness of need, and invitation from God. First, safely tucked inside most churches (sometimes all too safely) are people with valuable gifts, talents, and skills that are latent—hidden. Most often these people and their skills remain inactive not because of laziness or selfishness, but because they lack a clearly defined sense of how their particular skills can contribute to the mission of the church. Second, most churches, even those with only a rudimentary understanding of their immediate surroundings or the wider world, are not insensible to the needs that exist around them. In fact, the immensity of the need sometimes leaves them paralyzed, not knowing where to begin. Because of the challenges inherent in defining a focused, goal-oriented, measurable way to engage with specific needs, many churches feel adrift in the sea of needs around them. When any effort at all seems like a drop in such an ocean of need, sometimes they decide to make no effort at all. Third, it must also be acknowledged that most churches are profoundly aware of God's call or invitation to engage. In most churches, congregants are (hopefully) exposed each week to a carefully crafted message articulating that call to engage the world in some way. This week-by-week exposure to the call of God can sometimes lead to a distracted lack of focus or discipline. With each new sermon, with the introduction of a new call to obedience, churchgoers are reminded of their shortcomings in a given area and renew yet another short-lived commitment to evangelism or mercy or purity.

The challenge, therefore, is not simply to be aware of talent, need, and call, but to see the places where all three intersect. This point of convergence is the ideal genesis for justice ministry.

Spiritual Preparation

Before you jump into the specific tasks related to exploring your church, community, and world, it is important to remember that you will be dealing with deep spiritual realities. While there is much more that could be said about these spiritual truths, it is important to remember that the evil your Justice Task Force will explore actively resists being brought into the light. It is vital, therefore, to remember that the work of justice has always been God's work, and if you plan to join God in it, you should spend some time in spiritual preparation.

As your Justice Learning Community transitions into a Justice Task Force, we strongly encourage you to spend your first meeting (and regular time at subsequent meetings) praying for the following four things that don't come naturally. As your Justice Task Force works together, it will be increasingly essential to live and work out of these four postures:

1. *Humility*—Remember that your team does not have all the answers. You are not called to be crusaders crushing injustice wherever it rears its ugly head. That work is God's. Ask God to lead you into the necessary humility.

2. *Wisdom*—God wants to give his children all the wisdom they need (James 1:5). What do you imagine needing wisdom for in this process? How will you invite God and others he has gifted as wise counselors into your discernment process?

3. *Love*—Ask God to cultivate love in you for the victims of injustice you will discover. Some are people who are nearby and perhaps familiar to you. Others are far away and perhaps unfamiliar and unlike you. But these are the real neighbors God calls and equips you to love.

4. *Hope*—Pray against the temptation to despair that you will undoubtedly feel as you encounter the people you'll be serving and contemplate the injustices they suffer. Remember as you share with each other and with the wider church that it will take about nine units of hope to counteract every unit of despair-inducing injustice you uncover or relate. Be studious and disciplined about finding and communicating hope even in the darkest places.

Prayer, of course, as both hard work and desperate refuge, is foundational to the work of justice. In fact, because it is so essential, an entire section on prayer is included as part of the Engage phase. Feel free to turn there now (pages 194–197) for some ideas as you weave prayer into the experience of the Explore phase.

Explore Your Church

The healthiest, most obvious place to begin your exploration will be right at home. It will be essential for you to know and understand your own church community before you focus your efforts on the outside world. As a Justice Task Force, you need to develop a plan to address several important questions. Some of the questions will involve simply gathering data about your congregation; some will require you to explore the ministries and departments of your church and even your philosophy of ministry in certain areas. The process often yields surprises that are both encouraging and challenging. But given a commitment to prayer and to working with church leadership, the process universally yields helpful results.

In the following pages, you will find a set of specific questions to get you started. Begin mulling over these questions as a team. Assign an "owner" to each one, someone who will take the responsibility of formulating a plan to explore and answer each question for your church. These owners are not necessarily responsible to do all the work themselves but to lead the team in seeing that the work is done to thoroughly answer each question. You may, of course, add questions to this list yourself. Each question is followed by a number of suggested action steps to get you started. Your Justice Task Force will quickly become the experts on how best to answer each question for your church. Again, these action steps are offered simply as a beginning. Feel free to modify and add to the action steps in each category.

Not to Be Served, but to Serve

As you begin interacting with leaders and key volunteers in your church, please be careful to remember a few basic things.

First, remember that the lay leaders and staff of most churches are already working hard to accomplish a significant amount, often with limited resources. Most of them are in their positions because they love the church, and some have made financial or career sacrifices to take their positions. They have full schedules and most regularly must say no to opportunities that arise. If your Justice Task Force has been well led and has come through an effective Encounter phase, they are likely full of energy and passion to see the entire church and all of its ministries fully embrace God's call to justice. It will be very helpful for Justice Task Force members to pause for a few minutes and put themselves in the shoes of the lay leaders and staff they are responsible to talk to. It is vital to approach church leadership with the right attitude.

It's important to remember that the goal of the Explore process is not to ferret out the places where your church is failing or falling short in the work of justice or to chastise yourselves or your church leaders for any gaps you may discover in your ministry programming. Neither should you assume that the leaders you approach do not care about the issue of biblical justice. Be careful to treat church leaders the way you would want to be treated if you were in their position.

Perhaps it would be helpful to consider IJM's three core values as you approach staff and ministry leaders. IJM has a simple set of three values that govern our approach to everyone we interact with, from our colleagues, to the wider body of Christ, to our clients, to public officials, and everyone in between. These values are that we seek to be Christian, professional, and bridge-building in all that we do. These are simple, but consider each one briefly. What would it look like if you were to approach church leaders while embodying the following values?

- *Christian.* In all that we do, we seek to be inspired by Jesus. We seek not to be served, but to serve. We seek to be humble and grateful. We seek to be submitted to the Father in all things. We acknowledge that the work of justice is God's work. The church itself is God's. God cares far more about these things than we ever could. And we seek to be dependent on the Holy Spirit, prayerfully seeking wisdom in all we do and seeking to display the fruit of the Spirit.
- *Professional.* We engender, earn, and keep trust. We are disciplined; we value knowledge and expertise. We demand accuracy and dependability (especially of ourselves). We keep commitments. We follow through. We evaluate by outcomes. We love to learn.
- *Bridge-building.* We seek common ground and build relationships and partnerships from there. We are humble in our perspective and in our interactions with others.

If you are careful to engage with love, humility, wisdom, and hope, and if you insist on operating out of a set of core values that are Christian, professional, and bridge-building, then your engagement with the leadership of the church cannot help but be constructive. You will approach leaders with a sense of gratitude and appreciation for what they are already doing. Any questions you have connected to the Explore process will be brought with humility. And the result will be that church leadership will feel served and cared for in the process.

Questions for Your Justice Task Force to Consider
1. Is your church a safe place for victims of injustice already in your midst?

The very first place you need to explore justice is in your own homes and church communities. Consider this: the generally accepted statistics are that nearly one in five women in the United States is raped or assaulted in her lifetime, and an even higher rate (one in three) experiences physical abuse from a husband or partner at some point.[1] It is a sad and simple statistic that grave injustices such as sexual abuse and domestic violence exist in many (if not most) churches in the United States. The work of justice must begin at home if you are to engage with integrity anywhere else.

Action Steps

- *Is your congregation knowledgeable about issues of domestic violence and sexual abuse?* If not, consider how this important educational work should be done. Teach about these subjects from the pulpit, in premarital classes, in church bulletins, and in Sunday school. Ensure that leaders in the church receive appropriate training to respond to these issues if and when they arise.

- *Do your church staff and children's ministry workers understand mandated reporter laws and best practices in your state?* These laws differ significantly from state to state. Some local governments treat clergy as mandated reporters of child abuse, some do not. It is important to understand your role and obligation under the law. An excellent place to begin this research is the US government's Child Welfare website (www.childwelfare.gov). Among other things, this site contains a report titled "Clergy as Mandatory Reporters of Child Abuse and Neglect: Summary of State Laws."[2]

- *What does your church currently do to acknowledge and support survivors in your midst?* Commit to making your church (and home) a sanctuary where victims of abuse can find help, support, and healing.

- *Does your church offer concrete services to survivors of any forms of injustice or oppression?* If not, develop a plan to provide support to any survivors who choose to identify themselves. There are excellent resources, national ministries, and conferences that excel in the work of survivor support and aftercare. Consider setting aside funding for the counseling and aftercare of victims of domestic violence and sexual abuse in your congregation and perhaps in your community as well. Let congregants know that material support exists for those who may need or desire it.

- *Is your church vocal about these issues?* This is an obvious challenge for church leaders, but it can be done. Speak out against issues like sexual abuse, domestic violence, and rape from the pulpit, remembering to take into account the pain and vulnerability of the survivors potentially sitting in the congregation. Church leaders have a powerful impact on the attitudes of their congregations with respect to these issues. If the leaders talk about them in a sensitive and appropriate way, it will give permission for survivors and other concerned congregants to do the same.

- *Does your church show up when the larger community is talking about these issues?* It can be challenging to navigate the various ways communities speak out on these issues, but appropriate participation by church members and church leaders makes a powerful statement about your church being a safe place for victims and survivors. Find out who is talking about these issues in your community. Consider how you might join them.

- *Is your church aware of members or attenders who are involved with the court/probation system? Is there anything the church could do to better support families of inmates or those recently paroled?*

- *Are members of your church or group volunteering with*

local domestic violence and sexual abuse service providers? If not, lead by example. Consider volunteering with a rape crisis hotline or becoming a volunteer victim advocate[3] in your church and/or community. Seek ongoing training to ensure you are equipped to respond to such crises.

- *Does your church deal openly and holistically with the issue of pornography?* All too often, churches view the use of pornography exclusively as sin in the "personal purity" category. And if it is dealt with at all, it is discussed only in "safe" places like men's retreats.

  While clear data is still very difficult to find, what can be said with confidence is that users of pornography cannot always be one hundred percent sure of what they are looking at. They cannot determine that all subjects in the images and videos they view are consensual adults. It would therefore be prudent to assume that the burgeoning porn industry, to some degree, overlaps with the world of human trafficking and commercial sexual exploitation of women and children.

  Connecting the dots regarding pornography's role in the abuse of women and children often powerfully motivates repentance for those who struggle with sin in this area. Repentance will involve changing people's thinking about pornography as a victimless, private sin—it is also an issue of justice. Those who struggle with pornography (and those who love them) need to understand the issue from both a personal purity perspective *and* a justice perspective. Consider doing some research and producing a curriculum connecting these issues in a way that could serve those struggling in this area.

2. What are the latent skills in your congregation?

There are likely members of your congregation whose education and professional experience have afforded them specific skills that will be great assets to your church as you explore involvement in justice work. People with experience in law enforcement, to name just one example, are immensely valuable in this process. Sadly, these same people often feel like their skills and experience do not relate directly to the work of the church. Often these skilled professionals end up attending church on Sunday morning but engaging very little beyond that. Because they tend to be low-profile, you may not even know they are there! You need to do some work to surface these valuable people before you proceed any further. Along the same lines, does your church have lawyers, medical personnel, social workers, counselors, artists, musicians, project managers, people with business development experience, spiritual directors? All of these will be valuable to the work of justice in your church.

Action Steps

- *Consider hosting a screening of a documentary on modern-day slavery followed by a discussion on the topic.* (Visit www.ijm.org for resources.) Specifically invite the people in these "latent" categories and cast a vision for how their expertise is necessary to the church in its fight for justice. As appropriate, you may want to invite some of these people to participate in your Justice Task Force.
- *Consider conducting a survey of the congregation.* Leaders are often surprised and delighted by what a congregational survey reveals. Significant skills and talents may lie hidden regardless of the size of the church in question. This information can be revealed through something as simple as a brief survey executed

on paper forms during a Sunday morning worship service. Alternatively, surveys can be conducted using many of the online tools that exist. Some churches may want to consider a deeper dive into the question of talents and skills by encouraging their small groups or ministry teams to use an assessment tool such as Clifton StrengthsFinder.[4] Regardless of how you choose to do this, it is an important step of obedience. Jesus clearly teaches that you have been given talents and skills in order to light up the world. Lamps that are hidden under baskets (or in church pews) do nothing to shine light into dark places (Matthew 5:14-16). Consider distributing the short survey on page 164 asking individuals to identify their willingness to learn more and potentially engage in the newly forming justice ministry.

3. Is your church giving financially to the work of justice?

Jesus said it, but we're often reluctant to believe it: the stark biblical truth is that our hearts tend to follow our money. Giving, therefore, will be a great way to explore involvement in the work of justice. Take a look at your church's ministry budget. What does the basic pie chart look like? Most church ministry budgets stretch to include funding for efforts in church planting and evangelism. Some go so far as to include ministries of mercy[5] among the projects they fund. Very few churches, however, have made a financial commitment to the work of justice. In 2005 IJM did a basic analysis of the financial statements of 517 Christian ministries. It was quite illuminating. The analysis revealed that Christians gave $5.6 billion per year to evangelism and church planting and $9.4 billion to relief and development. Comparatively, during the same period, Christians gave almost

CHURCH GIFTS AND SKILLS SURVEY

Please answer the following questions to help us identify the skills and gifts present in our congregation as we move forward in the work of justice.

Name: _____

E-mail address: _____

Age: ☐ 0–18 ☐ 19–25 ☐ 26–40 ☐ 41–64 ☐ 65+

Status (please check all that apply)**:** ☐ Student ☐ Single ☐ Married
☐ Young kids in the home

Professional skills (please check all that apply):
☐ Administrative skills
☐ Advocacy
☐ Artist (Type: _____)
☐ Construction
☐ Consulting
☐ Counseling
☐ Event planning
☐ Grant writing
☐ Language skills (Language(s): _____)
☐ Law enforcement
☐ Lawyer
☐ Medical experience (Type: _____)
☐ Organizational skills
☐ Paralegal
☐ Project management
☐ Psychologist/psychiatrist
☐ Public speaking
☐ Research analyst
☐ Social worker
☐ Spiritual development
☐ Videographer
☐ Web developer
☐ Other skills: _____

Next steps:
Yes! I would like to volunteer with the **Justice Task Force**. Please contact me.
┈┈⇢ I am available to volunteer _____ hours per week.

Unfortunately, I cannot volunteer at this time. But . . .
☐ Please ask me again *later* when more tangible action items come up.
☐ Please keep me updated about how I can contribute *financially*.
☐ Please keep me informed about how I can *prayerfully* support the work
of justice.

nothing to the work of biblical justice.[6] Work with your church staff to carefully consider changing this.

Action Steps

- *Invite your church to pay for the rescue the poor cannot afford.* There are many ways your church can contribute financially to the work of biblical justice around the world. Because fund-raisers are effective at raising awareness, churches have been quite inventive and have come up with lots of interesting and exciting new ideas. Some have hosted dinners or sporting events; even a book study can become a fund-raiser.[7]
- *Make justice a church budget item.* Many churches have made the work of mercy an ongoing budget item, but relatively few have committed to funding the work of justice. Have your Justice Task Force explore the budget of your church and suggest ways to make a budgetary commitment to biblical justice.

4. Is your church passionate about a particular part of the world?

Do you send short-term teams to a particular part of the world each year? If so, God may have uniquely prepared your church to explore and perhaps meet justice needs in a specific community. While your church may already be addressing suffering caused by deprivation—those suffering for lack of basic needs or for lack of understanding the basic story of redemption—in the communities you serve, there may be an opportunity for you to add a ministry of justice to the good work you are already doing.

Action Step

Explore the places where your church is already involved and the people passionate about these areas. Your Justice Learning Community can assess whether there are leaders and participants in these trips who would be interested in exploring the justice issues that exist on the ground in these countries or communities. You may want to make these leaders aware of *As You Go*, a DVD resource from IJM that helps churches integrate an exploration of injustice into their ongoing work in mission settings around the world.

5. Is your church preaching about biblical justice?

If the church is to be fully captured and activated for the work of justice, then at some point the message will need to come from the pulpit. For many churches, this important step begins previously in the Encounter phase. But what sometimes happens is that groups of leaders within the church develop a passion for justice that does not yet exist at the higher levels of leadership and therefore is not reflected in the preaching. Sometimes the Justice Task Force has the challenging task of respectfully "leading up" in order to fully infuse all levels of the church with passion for justice. This can involve creatively and respectfully presenting opportunities for leaders to be exposed to the reality of injustice and the many tools that are available to church leaders as they learn and teach about biblical justice.

Action Steps

- *Encourage and equip the church staff to preach a sermon series on biblical justice.* Again, for many churches in the Explore phase, this has already happened or this task has been performed by a visiting IJM speaker. If the message of biblical justice has not yet come from the pulpit of your church, you should carefully consider how to make that happen. Perhaps encouraging your own pastor to preach on biblical justice is the best way to accomplish it. (To get you started, IJM provides free justice sermon outlines at www.ijm.org.)

- *Consider attending a key event together.* If at this point in your journey toward developing a justice ministry there are still key staff or volunteers at the church who need to be brought on board, consider inviting several of them to a significant event or conference where they will be immersed in and educated on the reality of injustice. (One such event I would recommend is IJM's Global Prayer Gathering, held each year in the Washington, DC, area.[8]) This could be just the kind of exploration your church is ready for.
- *Provide books and resources to your pastor or other key church staff.* Some readers of this book will be pastors looking for ways to engage their congregations in justice ministry. But some readers will be congregants seeking to engage their *pastors* in justice ministry. If you are in this second category and are seeking to influence your pastor, you may want to consider passing along a book. Pastors who are required to preach forty to fifty times per year are constantly reading. In an effort to hone their craft, they ingest a steady diet of books on all sorts of subjects. I have included a list of books on justice in Appendix 1. If you're looking for a basic primer, I would encourage you to consider one of the books written by IJM's president Gary Haugen: *Good News about Injustice*, *Terrify No More*, or *Just Courage*. Consider providing a copy of a key book for your pastor and including a note that describes what was helpful or interesting to you and why you think it might be relevant for your pastor and your church.
- *Screen a movie for your staff.* Any one of the short IJM documentaries available at www.ijm.org or IJM's Vimeo site at http://vimeo.com/ijm would serve as excellent educational tools for church staff and volunteers. You may

also consider screening a longer movie like *Call + Response* (www.callandresponse.com) for your staff.

This list of questions and action steps is intended to serve as a starting point for your Justice Task Force. As you move through the work of answering these questions, undoubtedly more and perhaps better questions will arise. It is important that the leader of the Justice Task Force help the team carefully accommodate these new questions and track their work as they begin to discover answers. The use of a simple table or spreadsheet may be a good place to begin. Then, as the work on each question matures, the "owner" of that question should assemble a report on what the team investigating the question is learning. Inevitably the team will discover some gaps in the church's ministries and vision. But you will also discover rich areas of resources and creative ways your church is responding to needs you didn't even know about. Inevitably the process of exploration leads to a deeper love for the

[Church Name] Justice Task Force

Leader:
Members:

	Question	Owner	Action Steps
Explore Our Church	Is our church a safe place for any victims of injustice already in our midst?	Jim Martin	1. Conduct basic web research to determine level of victimization in our church and community. 2. Interview pastor of healing ministries . 3. Meet with domestic violence unit of local police. 4. Talk to staff about our church's premarital curriculum—are the issues of domestic violence and sexual abuse dealt with?
	What are the latent skills in our congregation?		1. Conduct a Sunday morning survey (simple paper ballot) over the course of two Sundays. (Begin with survey in book and work with staff to see if there are other questions we should be asking.)

church as you discover the great strengths inherent in your own congregation and experience the responsiveness of congregants and leaders seeking to embrace the call of God to the work of justice.

The chart below may be helpful as you begin tracking the work of the Justice Task Force. I've begun to fill in some of the lines as an example of what you might want to track.

Explore Your Community

With the process of exploring your church under way, soon it will be time to turn your attention to the community around you. As you consider doing this, a few words on how churches should approach their communities will be helpful.

As you move to action, you will do well to remember that many people outside the church are not accustomed to seeing the church involve itself in the important social issues affecting

	Target Completion Date	What Did We Learn?	Next Steps
	June 19		

the community. You may encounter some residual resentment from professionals in the community who have been fighting these battles for a long time. Many of them have long assumed that these issues *should* matter to the church and have been non-plussed at the church's seeming indifference. They have experienced the church as either utterly silent and completely absent from the places where these battles are being fought or bewilderingly obtuse when they did become involved.

The God of the Scriptures is neither silent nor absent, and neither should the people of God be. But you must proceed with caution and with the humility, wisdom, love, and hope that are the basic building blocks of Christian character (see page 155). You should be praying that the Father will continue to hone these character traits in you as you engage in this work of justice. Learning what the professionals in your community are already doing will be both inspiring and humbling. You will have to ask repeatedly for the wisdom necessary to discern your path through all that you will discover and learn. Perhaps you will even discover that repentance for the church's indifference will be the first and most important step. You should pray that love and hope will be the hallmarks of your engagement with both victims of injustice in your community and those who courageously serve them. As your Justice Task Force continues to meet, set aside time at the beginning of each meeting to discuss the role that humility, wisdom, love, and hope play in the work you are doing together. Discuss how the core values of Christian, professional, and bridge-building (see page 158) are best put to use. Pray together that God would deepen these attributes in you and your teammates.

Your basic approach to exploring the community will be similar to the approach you used in exploring the church. What follows is a list of questions and suggested action steps that will get you started. Again, each question will need an "owner" who will take responsibility for formulating a strategy to answer the question and reporting on the results. The research required in this section will be more complex than that required in the previous section. If your Justice Task Force doesn't have enough members, you may consider recruiting a few more people at this point. Often Internet research and reading are things that can be done very well by students and at-home parents. Students can sometimes weave this research into their schoolwork, and at-home parents often enjoy an opportunity to contribute to the ongoing work of the church that doesn't require additional meetings and the need for babysitters, and that can come during a time when they can feel isolated and in need of some intellectual challenge.

As you read through this list, think about strategies for mobilizing your Justice Task Force to explore all these categories.

1. What are the basic statistics that tell the story of injustice in your community?

Familiarize yourself with the statistics on violence in your community—especially violence against chronically vulnerable people. This data can be overwhelming, so it may be helpful to focus on a few specific categories as you begin. What data can you unearth regarding rape, domestic violence, child abuse, prostitution, sex trafficking, labor trafficking, and treatment of immigrants and prisoners in your area? What are the trends in these statistics over the last ten years? What do you learn from this?

2. What are the likely places of violent abuse in your community?

Are the crimes that generate the above statistics spread evenly over your community, or are they more prevalent in certain geographic areas? Make a map of what you discover. Is there a significant homeless population? Are the homeless disproportionately victims of violence in the community? Do other economic, social, or ethnic groups show up disproportionately as victims?

3. Talk to social workers in your community.

Often overworked and underappreciated, social workers are personally aware of many of the justice issues in your community. If there are social workers in your church, invite them to speak to the Justice Task Force about their experiences with injustice in your community.

4. Talk to the police in your community.

Law enforcement personnel are generally encouraged when they know that citizens appreciate them and are on their side. Spend some time exploring the website of your local police department. Look for the officers or departments dealing with violent oppression. Often these officers are delighted to talk with concerned members of the community. Consider inviting an officer to speak to your Justice Task Force (you may want to try specifically to connect with the officer or departments assigned to human trafficking, domestic violence, vice, or truancy). Remember that it is very easy to underestimate the value of getting to know the police officers in your area. Specific officers are often assigned to liaise with the community at neighborhood association meetings. Some precincts host community open houses themselves. Find out the ways your local police force is reaching out to the community and show up there. The relationships you develop will be an asset to your Justice Task Force.

5. What people and agencies are working for justice in your area?

Using information from these conversations, build a list of the public and private agencies in your community. Locate them geographically on your map. Assign a person from the Justice

Task Force to research each agency, learning as much as possible from the web and other sources. While a significant amount can be learned through web research, some of the most valuable information will come from direct interviews with these service providers. If possible, conduct a personal interview with the relevant staff person of each agency you are researching. Be very careful and open to explain the purpose of your visit, that you are gathering information on the organizations working to provide services to victims of violence and injustice in the community. Be sure to maintain a careful list of the contacts you have made at each agency. The web of relationships you are building will be at least as valuable as the information you gather.

6. What issues of injustice are these agencies confronting?

As you catalog each agency, be sure to note each organization's area of focus or expertise and how long they have been working in a particular area. Also include an assessment of which injustices are being met by strengths in the agencies and services you are discovering and which injustices fall into "service gaps" or weaknesses in the community.

7. Educate your congregation about the extent of these issues.

Violent injustice is hard to look at. The biblical call to love your neighbors must begin with a willingness to understand and empathize with their plight. A vital step in this process will be for your Justice Task Force to strategize a variety of ways to educate your church about the issues specific to your community. This can and should be done not only from the pulpit, but through Sunday school classes, in small group Bible studies, through special seminars, through walking tours of your city, through imaginative short videos, and using any other creative educational approach your Justice Task Force can invent.

8. Do not forget the importance of hope.

While statistics about injustice may be easy to communicate, they can also be immobilizing for those who hear them. Consider the following:

- *Always offer education with opportunity.* Every time you communicate information about a particular injustice in your community, be sure to also offer something people can *do* about it, even if it is a simple thing. Often doing *something*—even something small—can keep learners from becoming paralyzed by despair. And taking these first small action steps can make a tangible difference in the lives of victims or those vulnerable to abuse. For example, if you share about violence in the homeless community, consider offering the opportunity to serve the local homeless population at a soup kitchen or by simply sharing sandwiches or blankets in the park. If you are communicating information

	Question	Owner	Action Steps
Explore Our Community	What statistics tell the basic story of injustice in our community?	Jim Martin	Research basic statistics on violent crime: 1. rape 2. child abuse 3. domestic violence 4. sex trafficking 5. labor trafficking 6. prison abuse
	What are the agencies working for justice in our area?	Jim Martin	1. Conduct basic web research to find local agencies.
	What issues of injustice are the above agencies confronting?		1. Develop an interview questionnaire for use while interviewing agency representatives. 2. Set up meetings with representatives at each agency. 3. Compile interview data.

about domestic violence in the community, offer the opportunity to participate in a work project at a local shelter.

- *Share success stories.* One persistent and pernicious lie is that the problems and effects of injustice are insurmountable. Exposing this lie brings hope. Be sure to share consistent stories of success and hope along the way. (Visit www.ijm.org for examples.) Work hard to discover and document stories of hope from work in your own community. Be disciplined about sharing these regularly.

Continuing the table you began on pages 168–169 will yield something like the one below.

You will also want to build a list of public and private agencies working in your area, including information about the focus of their work and their core competencies. A simple chart like the one on the following page might be a good beginning place.

Target Completion Date	What Did We Learn?	Next Steps

List of Agencies Working with Victims of Injustice in Our Community

[Church Name] Justice Task Force
Leader:
Members:

Injustice Category	Agency Name	Owner	Physical and Web Address (including contact name)
Domestic Violence	InnVision	Jim Martin	1900 The Alameda Suite 400, San Jose, CA 95126 408-292-4286 InnVision.org Contact:
	Next Door Solutions to Domestic Violence	Jim Martin	234 E. Gish Road, Suite 200 San Jose, CA 95112 408-501-7550 NextDoor.org Contact:
Rape			
Trafficking			

Services Provided	Strengths	Agency Contact
InnVision is perhaps best known for providing homeless and transitional housing services, but in at least two locations they provide excellent shared housing services to over 150 survivors of domestic violence through a program called HomeSafe.	The HomeSafe program is excellent and secure, seeking to provide safe transitional housing to survivors of domestic violence. They collaborate with Next Door (NextDoor.org) to provide onsite services and counseling to clients. I am seeking specific data on success rates and hope to have it soon.	Jane Doe JDoe@ email.net Jane is the volunteer coordinator for InnVision. She has a lot to teach us and would love to put our people to work. Also, she's very open to coming to our church to speak to the Justice Task Force or some other appropriate group.
Next Door seeks "to end domestic violence in the moment and for all time." Next Door promotes safety for battered women and their children through emergency shelter; multiple points of entry for victims; individual, system, and institutional advocacy; crisis intervention; education for victims and the community; and the changing of community norms through prevention activities. (From the mission statement page of their website)	The sense I got from talking to staff at Next Door is that they are authentic. I also love that they partner with other organizations to provide collaborative solutions to complex problems. They are a potential go-to source should we discover issues of domestic violence in our church that exceed our professional and pastoral capabilities.	

As you can see, it is often true that investigation of one service-providing organization will lead to other organizations doing helpful work in the same geographic area.

The work of exploring your community requires a significant amount of discipline, wisdom, and creative energy. While the information in this chapter is certainly enough to get you started, you may discover that your Justice Task Force would be better served by more specific instruction and guidance. For this reason, IJM has produced a Community Justice Assessment Tool. This tool is available free from IJM for churches participating in *Dive*. In it your Justice Task Force will find step-by-step instructions for completing a full justice assessment of your community. The entire process will take six to twelve months, but the resulting understanding you gain will be invaluable. You can find more details about this tool in Appendix 4 on page 253.

Explore Global Opportunities
Explore Your Own Global Networks
When you explored your congregation, you considered whether there were any areas of the world for which God has given your church a particular passion. If this passion has been expressed through mission trips, a long-term mission presence, or connections with organizations on the ground, this is a great point to consider the global network your church is already a part of. If your church sends teams internationally each year, then you have done the hard work of establishing relationships with trusted ministry partners and hosts. What you may not realize is that this global network you have developed is an extremely valuable asset.

Have your Justice Task Force create a list of all your international partners and key contacts. This list will be similar to the list of agencies you developed for your own community—you can even modify the chart on pages 176–177. The list should include a brief description of each partner and the nature of your church's relationship with them. Include current contact information for the organization and key points of contact within it.

Are any of your partners already engaged in justice ministry of some kind? Do any of your partners provide services that would be valuable to survivors of injustice? You may be surprised by the relationships that are revealed through this process.

Explore Frontline Organizations

As you do the work of educating yourself and your congregation and as you explore the issues of injustice in your church, your community, and your global networks, you will also want to gain a deeper understanding of ministries and organizations already conducting justice work around the globe. I mentioned earlier that the church's global investment in justice is dwarfed by investments made in other areas of ministry. While this remains true, the great amount of growth over the past decade in this area is heartening. Brand-new ministries as well as new areas of focus in established organizations have created new avenues of frontline response to the needs of vulnerable people who have become victims of violent oppression.

Have your Justice Task Force explore global frontline ministries, asking a set of specific questions about each organization (you can create another form like the one on pages 176–177 to record your research):

- What is this organization's mission?
- What is the organization doing to accomplish its mission?
- How does the organization raise awareness and advocate for change?

- Does it provide direct services to victims? If so, what services are provided?
- Does the organization engage in preventative services to reduce vulnerability?
- How does the organization handle the perpetrators of violence?
- Where does the organization work?
- What is the organization's impact?

I hope you'll explore the work of IJM during this phase. Our website—www.ijm.org—is a great place to start. You'll be able to find information on how and where IJM works, our latest results in bringing rescue to victims of slavery, sex trafficking, and other forms of violent oppression, and breaking news from our field offices. You can also get information on *Dive*—our program to support churches through the Encounter, Explore, and Engage phases.[9]

Proceed with Wisdom

We began this section with a discussion of three intersecting circles—the place where the church's unique talents, a specific unmet need, and the call of God all overlap. Your Explore phase—finding real neighbors to love and concrete ways your church's gifts and skills can be deployed to combat injustice—will reveal many talents in your church and likely uncover several significant unmet needs in the community. It will be important to consider these things carefully and prayerfully as you develop and add to the lists in both areas.

Especially as you discover unmet needs in the community—places where real neighbors are suffering and lack the support, services, and love of people from the community—you will feel a strong desire to engage immediately. This is the precise point at which wisdom is absolutely necessary. Remember, not every need—not even every compelling need—dictates a call from God to engage. This is why an intentional discernment process should be a part of your Explore phase. While your team should ask God for his grace in keeping the hearts and minds of your team attuned to his passion and voice throughout your process, a time of intentional, prayerful discernment can be a crucial step in receiving a clear sense of call from God directing you where to engage.

Reporting Your Findings and Discerning Direction

All the work of your Encounter and Explore phases will have surfaced many different tangible ways your church may be able to respond to God's call to justice. This work will also have surfaced pages and pages of documentation. Once the preliminary results are gathered, it will be time to summarize them in a research brief. Gifted researchers on your team will have no trouble creating such a document.[10] At this point, it might be worth considering another little celebration as you survey your work. There are still relatively few churches that have produced a document like the one you now have at your fingertips. This will also be an important point at which to check in with the wider church. The document you have produced will be of great interest to many in the congregation as well, even those who have not been close to the Encounter and Explore phases.

This is also the point in the Explore process during which gifted intercessors, members of your congregation particularly blessed with wisdom, and church leadership should come alongside the Justice Task Force. You'll want to gather wise, prayerful counsel as you seek God's direction through the massive pile of ministry possibilities you have discovered.

Sorting your findings into these three basic categories will be a helpful place to begin the discernment process:

1. *Has your Explore process uncovered any justice ministry in which your church is already engaged?* You will certainly want to pay close attention to this. If your church has already developed relationships with ministries involved in biblical justice, or if church staff and volunteers are already directly engaged in the work of justice themselves, you will want to come alongside and support what is already happening—especially if this is something that the church leadership has endorsed and still supports.

2. *As the Justice Task Force did their research, did members feel a strong pull toward any specific issues or opportunities?* This is another area you will want to pay close attention to. As I mentioned before, not every need determines a call from God to engage. The decision to engage must be a conscious and wise choice that is the product of discernment. But this process should take into account the feelings and senses of the people doing the research. The overall sense of the group will be an excellent place to begin a discernment process.

3. *As you consider the specific needs that didn't fall into either of the above categories, how do those opportunities intersect with what you perceive to be your church's unique abilities?* Perhaps you, or members of your Justice Task Force, are left with the feeling of wanting to engage in all of the needs you have discovered. And perhaps you are paralyzed by the realization that choosing one area of engagement means *not* choosing to engage all of the other needs you have worked to become aware of. What

do you do then? In this case, the best course of action is to prayerfully consider the list of needs and how it intersects with the abilities you have discovered or affirmed in your church. What are the strongest points of intersection? What are the weakest points?

From this point forward, discernment is a matter of praying for wisdom and making a decision. Sometimes the church can be prone to over-spiritualize moments like these. Certainly this decision will be an important one, but you must not allow the weight of this importance to crush you or blot out your reason or prevent you from taking action. Many churches have excellent processes for making such decisions. If yours does not, consider this simple discernment process:

1. Have your Justice Task Force and the supportive friends who have come alongside for this portion of the process commit to taking a few days (perhaps up to a week) to consider all the information you have uncovered thus far.
2. Each team member should commit to praying daily through the list of possibilities and attentively allowing God to steer toward the direction he wants you to go.
3. Set aside a day to fast. During the fast, ask God to grant you wisdom and clarity.
4. Then come back together and have each team member present what they have discerned.
5. Compare notes and make a decision.

At this point in the journey, you are well equipped to understand and begin responding to the real issues of injustice in your community. This awareness alone can feel like something of a burden and can strain the decision-making process. Remember that Scripture promises wisdom to the faithful if they but ask (James 1:5). You have come this far in the process with the help and guidance of a loving God who promises never to forsake you. It is time to step from belief into trust.

Questions to Consider

- In what ways might you feel tempted to let education be enough—be an end in itself? What other issues might keep you from taking action?
- In what ways might you struggle with too much momentum? What are the potential pitfalls of moving too quickly?
- Of the two challenges (too much inertia and too much momentum), to which might your church be more susceptible?
- What signs do you see that a sense of biblical conviction regarding justice has begun to take root in your own heart? In your church?
- How would you articulate the need for spiritual preparation in the Explore phase? What form(s) of spiritual preparation seem most helpful to you?
- How do you see your Justice Task Force embodying the core values of being Christian, professional, and bridge-building? Which seem to come naturally? Which are more of a challenge?

Snap here with your smartphone or visit the link for a challenge from Jim to explore the work of justice close to home.

www.tyndal.es/JustChurch9

CHAPTER 10

Engage: Moving from Fear to Faith

CHAPTER 6 BEGAN with a discussion of risk and its role in the development of faith. What I left out of that discussion is where fear fits into the picture. Clearly, risk involves fear. Contemplating risk triggers fear. Engaging in risk requires the management of fear. There is no way to take a risk without effectively dealing with fear. It seems that some people in the world actually enjoy fear. There are people in the world who find it *fun* to watch a horror movie or seek some sort of gut-wrenching thrill. But this is not the case for most people. So it seems appropriate that as we push toward our final stage and begin to consider how we will take the risk to engage in justice ministry, we ought to reflect on fear for a few moments.

I went skydiving once. It was years ago, back in my younger days. Jumping out of a perfectly functioning airplane was interesting from the perspective of understanding how fear works as we attempt something challenging or scary. I scheduled my jump about a week in advance with a local skydiving school. During the days leading up to the event, every time I thought about what it would be like (which was often), I would feel afraid. More precisely, I had a tingling sensation that I associated with fear. As I contemplated jumping out of the airplane, I was a little frightened thinking about how I would feel at the moment of truth. Would I have the courage to jump? Would I chicken out at the last minute?

When the day finally arrived, there were some surprises. The first was a long, *long* training session I was required to go through before I was allowed to don the jumpsuit and parachute. I was required to learn about prevailing wind directions, how to read a wind sock, how to cover and protect all my vital organs should I land in a tree, how to hit the ground appropriately (looking out at the horizon and not at the ground), how to roll backward, spring up, and then collapse the parachute before it could again fill with air and drag me across the ground. There was a lot of information, but it all seemed relevant and helpful. I listened carefully.

But the most complex set of instructions I received that day had to do with how I was to exit the airplane. The craft that would be transporting me from the earth's surface into the atmosphere was a small high-wing model (the wings were attached to the roof of the cockpit). In order to leave the plane safely (and not be struck by the stabilizer—the horizontal part of the tail section), I would have to follow this set of instructions very carefully:

1. With the right foot, step out of the cockpit and onto the very small platform over the landing gear.
2. With the right hand, reach and grab the middle of the diagonal strut connecting the wing to the fuselage.
3. Carefully cross the left leg in front of the right, stepping on the very outer edge of the small landing gear platform.

4. Transfer weight onto the left foot, lifting the right off the landing gear platform and allowing it to dangle in the air.

5. Grab the wing strut with the left hand and carefully slide both hands as far up the strut as possible.

6. Step completely off the landing gear platform.

7. Dangle momentarily in the 80+ mph wind while arching the back.

8. Finally, let go of the airplane . . . let go of the airplane!

As I was walked through these instructions a seemingly end-less number of times by the jumpmaster, I marveled at how many steps this simple maneuver would require of me. And again I wondered if I would have enough courage to go through with it once the plane was at three thousand feet.

After all the training, it was time to board the airplane. Soon I found myself dressed in a jumpsuit with a parachute strapped to my back, crouched where the copilot seat would have been in a normal aircraft of this size. I say where the seat *would have been* because both the seat and the door had been entirely removed in order to expedite the jumpers' egress. It was at this point I learned that of the three jumpers in the plane, I would have the pleasure of exiting the aircraft first.

As the airplane went into its climb and as I watched the ground receding and familiar objects shrinking to ant-like proportions, I was still wondering how I would respond when the moment of truth arrived. The feeling of fear was present and palpable. Soon the airplane leveled off and the jumpmaster gave the command. My time had come. As I turned toward the door and prepared to fol-low the series of steps that had been drilled into me, a strange thing happened. All of the time I had spent contemplating the jump I had felt a kind of fear—that tingling sensation—as I wondered if

I would have the courage at "go time." But when the time arrived, I wouldn't describe what I felt as fear. What I felt was more an intense concentration and focus as I followed the exit procedure I had learned and rehearsed so many times earlier that day. I was surprised by the force of the wind as I stuck my right leg and right arm out of the cockpit, but the momentary surprise only served to sharpen my focus. In the end, I was quite thankful that a somewhat complicated step-by-step procedure had been prescribed to get me safely out of the plane. I followed the procedure to the last step, where I was finally hanging white-knuckled from the wing strut, looking back into the eyes of the jumpmaster. On his command, I released the strut without hesitation and began my journey back to earth. It was glorious.

I share this story because it has become something of a lesson for me. The plain truth is that there is no way to engage in the work of biblical justice without experiencing and confronting fear. This is true simply because there is no way to be faithful to the call of Jesus without experiencing and confronting fear. But having a specific plan for how to confront these fears—specific action steps to take—can bring a remarkable focus. Such an action plan can make approaching the failure point much more manageable. Conversely, if we approach the failure point without having confronted our fears or with no specific plan, we may experience a kind of trauma that can make our recovery more difficult. In fact, we may lose our appetite for the failure point altogether. At the failure point, unexamined fear can take us out of commission, make us ineffective, and leave us feeling abandoned by the Father who is actually right by our side.

The skydiving experience led to a helpful realization. While it had been quite a fearsome thing to *contemplate* skydiving in the days leading up to the event, once the day arrived and I was sufficiently prepared to engage, fear turned to focus and I simply executed what I had been taught to do. This was especially true at the moment when I needed to exit the airplane and let go of the strut. I was able to do this not because I am a remarkably brave person; I am not. The point of the story is that the preparation and training I received equipped me to do something I would never have had the courage to do on my own. At the moment of truth, I focused on the procedure I'd learned and executed it step by step.

From Fear to Faith

As you transition to the Engage phase, it will be helpful to talk about any fears you have become aware of. By now you and your Justice Task Force will have contemplated many different options for engagement. Most likely, you experienced some fear as you contemplated specific engagement possibilities—as you weighed and measured particular risks. It is important to give voice to these fears. Often the simple act of voicing them will drain their power. And what many Justice Task Forces have learned is the same truth I learned on my skydiving adventure: *contemplating* a risk turns out to be much more fearful than taking the well-prepared steps of *engaging* in it.

Fear is a funny thing that way. Often what we fear is simply the unknown. But as we break the unknown down into bite-size pieces, as we study it and plan to engage it specifically and directly, fear becomes focus and we begin to execute the engagement opportunity God has put before us. Careful training and preparation are precisely what makes engaging in the action possible.

There are several places in the Exodus account where the Israelites experience great fear. One that has always stood out to me is a fascinating scene that occurs in the middle of the story in Exodus 14. After all of the interactions between Moses and Pharaoh, after all the plagues, after all Pharaoh's recalcitrance and changes of heart, the Israelites finally leave Egypt. At one point as the mob of former slaves is walking through the desert, God tells them exactly where to set up camp—right on the edge of the Red Sea.

Meanwhile, Pharaoh has had yet another change of heart and decides he never should have let the Israelites go. He gathers his army and gives chase. The former slaves find themselves exposed and unarmed, pinned against the Red Sea with no escape. The situation is hopeless. They are pitted against Pharaoh's state-of-the-art fighting force complete with the latest weapons and war machines. Quite understandably, when the Israelites look up and see the Egyptian army advancing on them, they experience "great fear" (Exodus 14:10). So as the scene begins, the Israelites are, quite rationally, afraid of the Egyptians.

What follows is the story most of us learned in our childhood. Pinned down against the Red Sea by an Egyptian army pursuing them in deadly earnest, the Israelites say to Moses, quite sarcastically, "Was it because there were no graves in Egypt that you have taken us away to die in the wilderness?" (Exodus 14:11). Moses encourages the people to stand firm and watch what God will do. Then, instructed by God, Moses lifts up his staff and raises his hand over the sea . . . and the water is swept out of the way. The Israelites pass through the Red Sea as if it were dry ground. And when the Egyptians (unadvisedly) try to follow them, the sea closes in over them.

We all know the story. But what has always fascinated me is the reaction of the Israelites. At the beginning of the scene, the Israelites are afraid. Generations of slavery do not prepare a people to fight for themselves, and seeing the enormously superior force bearing down on them must have been absolutely terrifying. So you might expect that after God delivers the Israelites there will be a period of giddy relief not just because they have escaped, but also because of the miraculous manner in which they have been delivered. And there may, in fact, have been a kind of giddiness involved in the celebration described in Exodus 15. But their first reaction is much more interesting—and sober—than that. The final verse of Exodus 14 puts it this way: "So the people feared the LORD and believed in the LORD" (Exodus 14:31). The story begins with the Israelites fearing the Egyptians; it ends with the Israelites fearing God—a sober expression of deepened faith. This experience of God's unambiguously miraculous power moves the Israelites from a self-focused fear (for their own well-being and comfort) to a much more profound faith-filled fear of the supernatural power their God displays as Deliverer. In short, they move from selfish fear to faith.

It seems clear to me from the Scriptures that Jesus never intended to offer us a life free from fear. In fact, the desire to be free from fear and insecurity can drive us to distraction in the worst sort of way. What I *do* think Jesus offers us is an entirely different experience of an entirely different kind of fear. At the intersection of our three circles—talent, need, and call—lies the opportunity to engage the work of God in the world in a unique way. How could the convergence of these three things not be a place that inspires some appropriate fear in us?

I've seen it happen again and again as churches proceed through the Explore phase. Talents surface that open up whole new vistas of possibility for church engagement. Exposure to the very real needs in the community or around the world infuses the process with vision and desire—vision for what just might actually be possible and desire to make an impact, to love real neighbors in a tangible way. As talent and need interact with each other, a tingling sense of fear and anticipation becomes palpable.

Then, as leaders continue to pray and discern their way through emerging possibilities, a sense of call from God emerges.

Once the invitation to engage specific skills and talents in a specific problem becomes clear, a whole new kind of fear tends to ripple through the team: a wholly appropriate holy fear that God has invited you into the work of justice in a specific way to serve a specific group of people that God loves dearly. When these three things converge, the inevitable hurdles and obstacles to developing justice ministry seem less daunting. The significant resource requirements, the enormity of the need, the complexity of the problem—all these things suddenly seem if not more manageable, then at least less important. At the convergence of talent, need, and call, you find the faith to say yes to God's invitation and embrace the risks ahead.

Contemplating engaging in some specific and tangible way is like thinking about jumping out of an airplane. It can lead you to wonder if you will have the courage when the time comes. But careful planning will help sort that out. The more you learn about your community and work your way through the possibilities for engagement, the more this fear will turn to focused energy as you take the first steps.

And because you are a normal human being, the thought of engagement in these issues can also fill you with a kind of self-focused (even selfish) fear. If you engage, will you be safe? Will you be accepted? Will you be effective? But as you engage, what often happens is that these natural, self-focused fears give way. But here the news is just as good for you as it was for the Israelites. If you muster the courage to be faithful, what you will witness is God's unambiguously miraculous power to rescue and deliver. When that happens, a whole new kind of fear enters your soul—an awestruck appreciation for the God of justice who is able to do immeasurably more than you could ask or imagine.

Diving In

Through the work of your Justice Task Force and their supportive discerning community, your church has now likely come to
a place where you are ready to address any fears that linger and
then to step into the issues you have identified at the confluence
of need, gifting, and calling.

At IJM we've walked with many churches through the
Encounter and Explore phases through *Dive*, the program we've
designed to support churches in the work of justice. Many of
them begin the process with a particular direction (or even a specific ministry end point) in mind. But more often than not, when
these churches arrive at the Engage phase, they find themselves in
completely unexpected and often new territory. They sense the
call of God to move toward a need they had never before seen
and engage that need with a talent they never knew they had.
One of the best parts of my job is getting to watch this surprising
process unfold. It continually reminds me of the beauty of the
church's diversity. God has made your congregation unique, and
as a result, it is unlikely that your plan to Engage will look just
like any other church's. That's why in this chapter I don't offer
an exact, point-by-point plan for every step you'll take next. The
desire for such a plan is completely understandable—believe me,
I've heard this from nearly every church that IJM has engaged
with on a deep level. But there is little that can compare with
the exhilaration of watching God step in and empower ministry
that you could never have ever imagined at the beginning. So
I'm *glad* it's not up to me to suggest to you what your ultimate
outcome will be.

While I can't tell you exactly what your engagement model
will look like, I *can* guide you by sharing some common practices
that are part of nearly all successful engagements. As I shared

earlier, most robust justice ministries will feature all three facets: universal, local, and global. We'll explore the role each of these facets can play in your church's justice ministry.

Praying for the Work of Justice

If you have come this far, it is likely because intentional prayer for the work of justice has been a part of both your Encounter and Explore phases. As you enter your Engage phase, let me encourage you again with the scriptural reminder that coming before God in prayer is not *supplemental* to the other work you may be doing—it is every bit as much the work as the other action steps you will take. A church that has entered the Engage phase should have an intentional plan for how they will continue regular intercession through the process of engagement and beyond.

The discipline of prayer is carefully woven into the rhythm of life in all IJM offices. At IJM Global in Washington, DC, each staff member begins the day with thirty minutes of "stillness" at their desks. This time is set aside as preparation for the work of the day. Some staff pray, some read Scripture, some simply sit in the presence of our loving and just God. Then, later in the day, we meet for corporate prayer, where any special concerns or praiseworthy items are brought forward for prayer. Devoting an hour a day to prayer is no accident, nor is it done merely out of discipline. The work of biblical justice both fuels and demands a kind of prayer that is more urgent and enduring than that produced by sheer discipline.

Prayer is the primary and essential form of engagement in the battle for justice. There are thousands of intercessors around the world who have learned this for themselves. They have engaged in the call to biblical justice primarily through their gift and service of intercession. Every Justice Task Force building a plan

to Engage should begin here. Here are some specific action steps
to consider:

- Build prayer for the work of justice into your church's
  regular prayer rhythms and structures. Does your
  church have a prayer team or prayer ministry that
  meets regularly to pray about concerns in your church
  or community? Think about equipping these teams to
  intercede in the work of justice. Do you have a corporate
  or congregational prayer during your Sunday services? Are
  you interceding on behalf of victims of injustice during
  this time? If not, consider incorporating these needs into
  these prayer structures that are already a part of who you
  are as a church. I know that we at IJM often have urgent
  prayer needs for which we deeply covet your prayer—and
  we have a variety of ways to get these prayer requests to
  you, from IJM's mobile app to our prayer communities.
  Rest assured that all frontline organizations will be
  encouraged by focused prayer on behalf of their staff and
  the clients they serve.
- Start a justice prayer community at your church. Perhaps
  God is specifically calling your church into even deeper
  engagement in the work of justice through the work
  of prayer. If so, you may want to create a new prayer
  group with a specific justice focus. Praying together is
  important: the issues of injustice that drive us to prayer
  often involve a kind of suffering that is challenging to
  contemplate alone. One prayer group meets faithfully
  the same afternoon each week at a coffee shop. Some
  churches have chosen to establish a specific justice prayer
  service each month. Carefully planned, these evenings can
  be a powerful place for believers to worship the God of

justice and cry out on behalf of victims near and far. (If
you are planning such an event, I do hope you will visit
www.ijm.org or another frontline organization's website
to learn about ways to include other urgent prayer needs
as well.)

• Join or plan a justice prayer event with others outside
your church. Every year, IJM brings together staff and
friends from all over the world specifically to pray for
the global battle against injustice at our Global Prayer
Gathering. We spend a weekend interceding for victims
of oppression, IJM's staff, and the many challenges
faced by both. Field office directors from all of IJM's
offices share specific needs in their casework around the
globe. The thing I love most about the GPG is that it
is a place where we recognize together that prayer is an
indispensable part of the work of justice. And choosing to
pray for a mission that matters so deeply can drive us into
God's presence with a kind of desperation that is good
for our faith. I think this is the reason that people who
love prayer love the GPG. It is a place where they can
spend a weekend entirely immersed in intercession with
other seasoned prayer veterans. But I think this is also
the reason that people who don't necessarily love prayer
also love the GPG. Many of the people who attend have
never been to any other sort of prayer gathering and don't
consider themselves prayer experts or even accomplished
amateurs. But for them, gathering to pray for victims of
injustice and those who invest their lives to protect them
simply makes sense. If you are interested in knowing
more, look on IJM's website for the most current
information on this year's gathering.

 Your church can also host your own prayer gathering

around issues of injustice. At this point in the process you have likely seen and heard much that urgently requires prayer. What might it look like to gather other members of your community—from local churches to ministries with a justice focus—for prayer? Plan a time (from an hour to a weekend) of focused prayer around specific issues of injustice.

Making Justice a Budget Item

One sign that justice ministry has become a significant priority in any church is that leaders have done the work of including justice in the church's budget. Jesus' words to us ring true: "Where your treasure is, there your heart will be also" (Matthew 6:21). If you sense a clear call from God to the work of justice, this call will permeate all of who you are as a disciple; if the call has permeated your church, it will permeate all of who you are as a body. Ask God to give you discernment for how he wants you to invest the resources he has given you in his work of justice.

Financial engagement in the work of justice can look different for every church. We see great diversity in the ways churches engage through giving. For some congregations, financial support is about encouraging individual members to make sacrifices so they can give personally to justice ministry. (Many of IJM's Freedom Partners—people who have made a monthly commitment to supporting our most urgent needs—report that they were encouraged to take this step through their church.) Some congregations hold a public fund-raising event like Run for Justice—major events like this can be a great way to expand the opportunity to engage in the work of justice to your broader community. Raising funds is often a great way to engage youth— it's an action step they can take no matter how old, and their passion is often infectious. One young girl in the mid-Atlantic region sells lemonade every year at her county fair so that she can donate the proceeds to free slaves.

As part of my work with IJM, I have conversations with churches and church leaders about the importance of prayer and financial giving all the time. Sometimes these conversations have a slight edge of impatience to them as leaders listen to the options. And at this point in the conversation, I'll sometimes be asked a question like, "Yes, of course, that's all very important, but what can we do *besides* pray and give?" While I understand the question and am very willing to answer it, I always feel it's a good idea to pause for a moment first and consider just how important prayer and financial giving are. Many churches today are used to investing their financial resources and their people in the same place. The idea of investing financial and human resources simultaneously has become something of a principle of sound modern mission. So this question often comes from a concern I very well understand on behalf of church leaders in general and mission pastors in particular.

When I served at The River, the place this thinking entirely broke down for us was with a wonderful ministry that for security reasons I will not name. This unnamed evangelical mission seeks to serve rural Muslim populations in North Africa through various holistic, Christ-centered community development projects. The organization mobilizes career missionaries, all with various and significant professional skills. Some are civil engineers and some are educators, but they all give their lives to the work and live for decades among the people they serve. They build water systems for entire villages and latrines for schools, and they conduct excellent educational initiatives. They are very well received by their communities. They somehow manage to be both very patient and very successful.

As you might imagine, an organization like this one seemed the perfect partner for us at The River. So why should our strategy of investing our financial and human resources break down in this particular case? Simply because the entire organization is made up of Spanish-speaking men and women from Central America. Almost three decades ago, these courageous brothers and sisters realized that of all the people on our planet, they were among the best suited to reach rural Muslims. To this day, if you manage to visit this ministry, the only languages spoken are Spanish, Arabic, and French. (Most of the missionaries speak all three.) For all their education and excellent (even world-class) professional skills, my city-dwelling, mostly monolingual friends from The River were not able to provide much hands-on help. The River did, however, joyfully support this ministry both prayerfully and financially for many years without ever sending a team to visit or to serve.

In a similar way, it is quite complicated for churches to engage directly in the work of IJM. This is true for several reasons. First, there is often very little direct service that anyone outside a victim's culture and language group can provide—particularly in the immediate aftermath of abuse. Second, survivors, who have been betrayed and abused by so many, are very hesitant to open up and trust strangers. Third, and one thing many people new to the work of IJM often do not realize, is that the vast majority of our staff are Christians who are *at work in their own countries.* While churches from all over the world do play very meaningful roles in IJM's work, they are usually dependent on months or years of relationship building.[1]

Recently I was having a conversation over lunch about this idea with another of my IJM colleagues, a former field office director. He expressed some disappointment about how churches are sometimes unwilling to engage with IJM at all if they cannot imagine having "boots on the ground" from the beginning of the process. In the conversation, I pushed back, gently encouraging my colleague to see it from the church's perspective—that there is an understandably strong desire to involve people holistically, not just in giving, not just in praying, but in direct service as well. My colleague was thoughtful, and eventually the conversation shifted to something else. Later that afternoon, I received the following e-mail from my colleague, who'd obviously been thinking more deeply about the subject:

> Jim, I agree with you. Ideally, "mission" engages all aspects of an individual Christian's life—providing opportunities for prayer, sacrificial giving, relationship, and direct service. Active engagement of the whole person is good. Loving our neighbor really is a whole-life commitment. Jesus said, "If anyone wants to find his life, he must lose it." The apostle Paul further developed this theme in his letter to the Romans: "Offer your bodies as a living sacrifice, holy and pleasing to God— this is your true and proper worship." As we move out in mission, clearly, there are no limits. We are to hold nothing back.
>
> But wouldn't it be ironic if this very good desire to be obediently and completely engaged in mission became a barrier to loving people where total and complete engagement simply was not realistic? If we were to cut off our love and service in situations where circumstances prevented relationship or direct service? For example, should we withhold our prayers and financial resources from the millions of children dying of malaria and dysentery in Africa because we are unable to personally deliver the medicine and wells that they

need to live? Should we deny the cries for help from the young girls enslaved in the brothels of Asia because there is no appropriate avenue for us to walk in relationship with those girls? Is this what Jesus wants? I do not think so. I think Jesus simply wants us to respond to the need as it presents itself. Yes, we must hold nothing back. But, no, we cannot demand that the need present the opportunity for total engagement before we respond. If prayer is what is needed, then we must pray. If it is money, then we must give. If it is friendship, then we must be that friend. If it is hours of service, then we must give that service. Just as there are no limits, there are also no prerequisites for love.

As the next chapter will demonstrate, there are many ways that churches can (and have) become involved in the work of justice both locally and overseas—despite great complexity and sensitivity issues. My colleague's excellent point, however, is that we should not make our personal involvement a prerequisite for our engagement. For those of us who take the Scriptures seriously, the call to engage is clear.

Taking Personal Responsibility

Many of us are vaguely aware that our choices as consumers can have unintended consequences for others in our globalized, modern world. Some of these choices may actually be contributing to the kind of slavery and injustice we seek to combat. It is important, therefore, that we come to a clearer understanding of our own participation in the problem through our purchasing choices. It takes care and sacrifice to demand goods with clean, slavery-free supply chains and to follow through by supporting companies that provide these goods. But by reducing demand for slave-made goods, we reduce the economic benefits of slavery for those who profit from it.

Our friends at SlaveryFootprint.org have created a tool that makes this much easier to do. By completing the interactive life-style survey at SlaveryFootprint.org, you can find out how many slaves may be involved in producing the things you eat, use, and wear on a daily basis. You can download their Free World app to tell brands you care about their supply chains and to tell retailers you're interested in slavery-free goods.

Local Engagement

All of the above having been said, there are many vital ways for churches and their individual congregants to engage locally—and I'm sure you learned about and explored some of them as part of your process already. The largest task in this category, of course, will be taking all of the work you did in your Encounter and Explore phases (particularly if you conducted a Community Justice Assessment) and making it doable—turning it into ministry. As you work to turn talent, need, and call into new justice ministry in your church, many opportunities for engagement will naturally surface. This is also where the work in your particular church becomes highly individualized. While this sometimes-complicated work is going on, there are other modes of engagement that will both support it and offer other activities for members of the Justice Task Force and the congregation to engage in.

Becoming a Justice Advocate

Justice Advocates (JAs) are vetted and trained volunteers who are deputized to speak, network, and coach churches on IJM's behalf. We have many JAs all over the country working with our church mobilization staff. These excellent volunteers extend the reach of IJM staff by:

- personally connecting with a broad range of churches, sharing the IJM message, and offering tools such as those outlined in this book;
- knowledgeably coaching churches through the Encounter, Explore, and Engage process; and
- representing IJM at church and conference engagements where IJM staff cannot be present.

IJM periodically holds regional Justice Advocate training to equip JAs for their work. To find out about training in your area, contact your regional church mobilization staffer or send an e-mail to churches@ijm.org.

Engaging through Influence

Leading Others in the Body of Christ

As I stated earlier, a shift in the church is under way as the body of Christ broadly awakens to God's clear passion for justice. In the introduction to the tenth-anniversary edition of *Good News about Injustice*, IJM president Gary Haugen wrote, "A transformation of stunning speed and breadth is altering the Christian community—a transformation that offers great hope for the body of Christ and the world. . . . What an extraordinary era in which to be alive! In this epoch God is mobilizing his people into perhaps the most robust and holistic witness of his love that the world has ever seen."[2] That you hold this book in your hands now is yet another piece of evidence for this shift.

As you engage in the work of justice in the world, you may sense God calling your church to join him in this work of transformation within the Christian community. If your church has been significantly impacted during your encounter with the God of justice, you may sense a call from him to impact other churches or leaders in your sphere of influence. In fact, you may discover that working to see this shift continue and even accelerate is a place of significant engagement for you. You may thrist for even greater theological depth and resources to ground you in this expanding movement. If so, you'll want to take advantage of the IJM Institute for Biblical Justice, which fuels this shift in the global church by resourcing Christian leaders who desire to use their influence to advance the cause of biblical justice. The IJM Institute for Biblical Justice also works to present IJM's mission and the message of biblical justice at leading Christian forums around the world and to publish theological and practical resources—like this book—on this subject. For more information on the work of the IJM Institute for Biblical Justice visit www.ijm.org.

Advocating for Victims of Violent Injustice

The concept of political advocacy can be a touchy one in many churches. For different reasons, Christians from various traditions are sometimes mistrustful of engaging in government processes and seeking to impact their outcomes. But the fact is that child victims of rape, slaves, and widows whose land has been stolen from them need others to advocate for them. The Scriptures offer a clear call for us to become a voice for those whom injustice and oppression render voiceless. For example, Proverbs 31:8-9 says, "Speak out for those who cannot speak, for the rights of all the destitute. Speak out, judge righteously, defend the rights of the poor and needy."

And it should be no surprise that the Scriptures record character after character in the biblical narrative engaging in precisely this kind of advocacy—with governments and authorities—on behalf of those suffering oppression, abuse, and disaster. Here are just a few examples:

- Joseph bravely advocates with Pharaoh. Interpreting Pharaoh's dream, Joseph boldly invites Pharaoh to consider carefully how he will respond. And ultimately this former prisoner convinces his powerful political leader to embark on a massive grain storage program in preparation for the coming famine. Because of Joseph's advocacy, Egypt and much of the then-known world survive the crisis (see Genesis 41–45).
- Moses, at God's insistence, repeatedly advocates with an angry and recalcitrant Pharaoh for the freedom of the Israelites. (This saga begins in Exodus 5.)
- The prophet Nathan effectively advocates with the king of Israel (King David). Nathan creatively and forcefully calls David out on his sinful dealings with Bathsheba and the murder of her husband, Uriah (see 2 Samuel 12).
- Nehemiah carefully approaches King Artaxerxes and advocates for a leave of absence so that he can travel to the destroyed Jerusalem and rebuild the wall. With astute political sensitivity, Nehemiah also manages to enlist Artaxerxes's financial and material support for his project (see the book of Nehemiah, especially chapters 1 and 2).

The list of biblical advocates also includes Isaiah, Jeremiah, Daniel, Amos, Esther, John the Baptist, Paul, and many others. Christian history is full of those who have followed in the footsteps of these biblical characters. Take, for example, the great Christian parliamentarian William Wilberforce, who said, "The grand object of my parliamentary existence is the abolition of the slave trade. Before this great cause all others dwindle in my eyes. If it please God to honor me so far, may I be the instrument of stopping such a course of wickedness and cruelty as never before disgraced a Christian country."[3] For Wilberforce, this was "a long obedience in the same direction" as he introduced an antislavery bill every year for sixteen years until it was finally adopted on March 25, 1807.

Today, churches, Christian leaders, pastors, and congregations can—and should—play a vital role in advocating for the voiceless. They can appeal to the US government and governments around the world to provide concrete assistance to victims of violence. This includes advocacy to improve local courts, police, and prosecution and to make grants to anti-trafficking and anti-slavery NGOs. Joining in these focused efforts is an excellent way to Engage in the work of justice.

This advocacy work is often much easier to do than people realize. In the United States, senators and members of the House of Representative from both political parties care what their constituents think. Further, they know and respect Christian leadership in their home communities and welcome relationships with church leaders. IJM's government relations department can help arrange appointments for church groups, pastors, and congregants to meet with legislators and their staff, either during their visits to their states or congressional districts or in Washington. Even the shortest meeting that is friendly, nonpartisan, informative, and clear about what the legislator can do is beneficial to the cause of justice here and abroad.

Consider the following specific options for advocacy-related engagement:

- IJM offers advocacy training for interested Christian leaders, students, pastors, and church groups who wish to join in our justice campaigns. We hold workshops on US legislation and policy that relate to the abuses suffered by our clients in Asia, Latin America, and Africa. You will find information about these ongoing training opportunities at www.ijm.org.

- IJM government relations staffers organize groups of Christian leaders around the country. IJM's justice campaigns have volunteer leaders in most states who have collected tens of thousands of postcards for their elected senators and representatives in Congress regarding anti-trafficking policy.
- IJM offers advocacy training for participants and an opportunity to meet with legislators in Washington, DC.

Engaging Globally

As you consider all the information and opportunity that the Explore phase surfaced in and around your church, you will undoubtedly feel a significant pull toward local engagement. The immediacy and proximity of the issues you face will help your team to power through the inevitable challenges of program design and partnership. One final word of encouragement I would offer is this: as hard as your team has worked to research and uncover opportunities for local justice ministry, your team should work just as diligently to find meaningful engagement in justice issues in the Two-Thirds World.

Obviously, given the often great physical and cultural distances involved, global engagement can be even more complex than engaging in your own neighborhood. The issues you've researched—from labor and sex trafficking to domestic violence, rape, and police brutality—exist all over the world. But the reality is that the poor are a disproportionately large percentage of the victims of such violence. And further, the poor make up a disproportionately large percentage of the Two-Thirds World's population. The plain statistical fact is that violent oppression, though it exists in its various forms all over the world, is orders of magnitude worse in the Two-Thirds World. We can and should offer our very best efforts to engage these issues locally, but we should also do all that we can to see that these issues are engaged among the world's poor who live largely outside the rule of law. Given the level of expertise necessary for this type of global engagement, many churches execute their global justice ministry via partnership with IJM or other qualified organizations already engaged in successful justice ministry in the area in question. (In the next chapter you'll see some ways that congregations have met direct needs globally.)

By now you've spent a lot of time reading this book. You've thought through the processes as they were described. You may have even gathered a team. But you may still be thinking, *Yeah, but what does this actually look like?* It may be helpful to read through a few stories of how this process has emerged for different kinds of churches. The next chapter contains several stories of churches who have developed robust justice ministries by working through the Encounter, Explore, Engage process. Some of them have taken on complex ministry tasks; others are still looking for the best fit. But each of their stories will assure you that the most exciting, faith-building part of the journey lies just ahead.

Questions to Consider

- Recall a time when you attempted to do something that made you afraid. What was that like?
- What were the things you feared as you considered engaging in the battle for justice?

- How have these fears changed as you have learned more about these issues and what it looks like to engage them?
- How might working out a careful engagement plan help manage any fear that you are feeling as you move toward engagement?
- How do you imagine your faith might grow as you embrace the risk of engaging in justice ministry?

Snap here with your smartphone or visit the link for a message from Jim on the amazing things that can happen in your church when you truly engage in the work of justice.

www.tyndal.es/JustChurch10

CHAPTER 11

Real Churches with Real Problems

BACK IN CHAPTER 2, I referred to the first-century church as a "church with real problems." By this I mean that the life-and-death struggle the first-century church found itself in serves as a stark contrast to the smaller annoyances that use the ocean sunfish strategy to grow out of proportion in our lives and churches. But these days I am very hopeful about the church. From my perspective of traveling and speaking on behalf of IJM, I interact with many churches that have a growing sense of courageous vitality, a growing willingness to go looking for trouble—real, injustice-related trouble of the kind that offers faith-maturing trials. It's a simple thing to say, but the churches I walk into see themselves as so much more than just buildings to house congregations. They seem to understand that the mission of the church goes far beyond our own healing and salvation. There is a palpable and growing sense that the church, as envisioned and inaugurated by Jesus, is hardwired to take on the epic battles of good and evil in our world and that as we say yes to Jesus and enter this struggle, we find life.

The stories you will read in this chapter are from churches who have answered a resounding and enduring yes to Jesus. Some are called out because they model one phase of the process clearly; others have been examples every step of the way. In every case, if you had the privilege of knowing these churches and their leaders, one of the first things you would notice is that rare coexistence of the two prerequisites I mentioned in the introduction: humility and courage. You will undoubtedly see both of these virtues woven into their stories.

As you read, please keep in mind that none of these stories describes a perfect trajectory toward justice ministry—we call these churches "models" because they represent just what the process looks like. There is always a lot to learn, and the journey is seldom without its setbacks. But God's grace to us lies in the fact that while our efforts are decidedly and merely human, God is pleased to work through us.

Lake Grove Presbyterian Church—Lake Oswego, OR

There has long been a focus on outreach ministry at Lake Grove Presbyterian Church (LGPC) in Lake Oswego, Oregon. This focus intensified in 1995, when the church partnered with World Vision to serve the Wolof people of Senegal. LGPC members Clay and Maggie Creps were personally involved in this mission for years, eventually developing close relationships with some of the World Vision staff. In 2001, one of the staff gave Clay a copy of Gary Haugen's *Good News about Injustice*. The book opened Clay's eyes to God's passion for justice. It was convicting for Clay, but it also provided him with a vision of how he could use his training and experience as an attorney to serve God. In response,

Clay and a friend taught an eight-week class about the book on Sunday mornings.

Shortly thereafter, LGPC invited IJM staff members to their church for a visit. In 2004, Clay became a Justice Advocate through a pilot program funded by the M. J. Murdock Charitable Trust in the Pacific Northwest. In the meantime, LGPC began another partnership with World Vision in Zambia. During trips to Zambia, several church members were able to visit IJM's office in Lusaka, Zambia. In the summer of 2005, Clay traveled in advance of the rest of the Zambia mission team and spent almost a week working in IJM's Lusaka office, interviewing potential clients and teaching at churches regarding property rights and wills.[1] All the while, Clay reported on his experiences to LGPC.

Clay's wife, Maggie, also developed a passion for the work of justice and discovered she could serve God through IJM's work. She became a Justice Advocate, learning about IJM's work in Guatemala and Bolivia. Looking to further support IJM's work, she spearheaded Portland's first IJM benefit dinner.

Both Clay and Maggie have highly valued attending IJM's yearly Global Prayer Gathering in Washington, DC. The chance to gather with hundreds of IJM supporters and field office directors from around the world in a time of sustained worship and prayer is rejuvenating for the couple. They return each year to Lake Oswego on fire to share the biblical call to justice with their community and to raise support for IJM's work.

LGPC's partnership with IJM has led to a greater focus on issues related to biblical justice among both the pastoral staff and the members. Having the issue pushed to the forefront by several involved members of the congregation has caused the pastors to include the concept of biblical justice more frequently in sermons and to incorporate it in the education curriculum. In particular, the director of youth ministries has initiated a program among both junior and senior high youth every May called "May Justice Reign" month. The high school youth go through the Justice Mission curriculum and listen to speakers on issues related to biblical justice. The congregation at large has also begun giving financially to IJM. Since 2006, IJM has appeared as a line item on the church's annual budget. Lake Grove's pastoral staff have also been at the forefront of advancing legislation to fight human trafficking in Oregon and have worked with IJM in training hundreds of Oregonians in justice advocacy.

Although initially it seemed Clay and Maggie were lone voices, with perseverance, patience, and love, they continued to bring IJM and the issue of biblical justice to the attention of the pastoral staff and the missions committee at LGPC. The concept gained momentum, and the result has been a church that is talking about biblical justice and that is increasingly having members take an active role in educating others about justice and taking steps to live out God's call.

Crossroads Church—Cincinnati, OH

Crossroads' involvement in justice ministry started when Brian Wells, then the church's teaching pastor, read Gary Haugen's book *Good News about Injustice* in 2004. Brian describes reading the book as a "mind-blowing experience" for a couple of reasons. Through the scriptural references in the book, he was drawn more deeply into the context of several familiar passages (he cites Matthew 23:23 as one of them) to discover a profound reference to God's passion for justice that had previously eluded him. The book also awakened memories of Brian's childhood. Not unlike my IJM colleague Pranitha, Brian had grown up the child of a physician serving among the world's most vulnerable. In the late 1960s, while Brian was still quite young, his family had lived in Nigeria, where they witnessed horrible atrocities associated with the Nigerian civil war (also known as the Nigerian-Biafran war). These early memories combined with the modern stories of atrocity and injustice described in the book allowed the scriptural call to engage injustice to come alive in a new way.

Brian and other leaders from Crossroads visited IJM's headquarters in Washington, DC, and met with the staff. This meeting helped foster a relationship between Crossroads and IJM and further ignited a desire for action. Wanting to share this message with the rest of the church, Crossroads' leadership staff invited Gary Haugen to speak to the congregation in the summer of 2005.

The congregation responded with a strong desire to get involved in the work of justice. The church funded the cost for IJM to explore the possibility of opening a field office in a country where Crossroads was already heavily involved in ministry. Beyond the very generous funding, a volunteer team of researchers and writers at Crossroads assembled a deployment briefing guide that became a vital document to all IJM staff deploying to the region. At the end of the exploratory period, IJM determined that a new office would not be the best response to the needs of the country. Though this could have been viewed as a setback on their justice journey, Crossroads pressed on.

Still desiring to combat sex trafficking, Crossroads began partnering with IJM's casework in South Asia. In the past two years, multiple leaders and volunteers from Crossroads have visited the region to better understand the work of IJM in the field.

In 2008, Gary Haugen spoke at Crossroads again, this time during an all-church event called Consumed. Gary spoke to the congregation about IJM's dependence on prayer. Since then, volunteers have been meeting regularly to pray specifically for the mission of IJM in South Asia. Further, in response to the

Consumed series, the people of Crossroads increased their giving to IJM, specifically funding aftercare work in South Asia.

Crossroads is focused on engaging the work of justice in three ways. First, they have focused their partnership energies on improving aftercare for victims of sex trafficking in South Asia. Their goal is to see victims of sex trafficking fully reintegrated into life and work following their rescue. Second, they are seeking to use the full range of talent the church contains. Artists, writers, researchers, marketers, and other professionals have all been actively involved in their work to end the sex trade.

Most recently, Crossroads has decided to invest even more deeply in South Asia. Identifying a significant gap in aftercare services, Crossroads created Crossover Foundation, a nonprofit organization seeking to engage and equip the local Indian church to create sustainable aftercare solutions. Crossover serves as a guide to Western churches, connecting them with reliable local partners on the ground in Mumbai and working as a team to mobilize the church in India to meet the need. So far, Crossover has mobilized two different Indian denominations to supply financial and human resources to create short-term housing for trafficking survivors. These efforts provide the services the survivors need most in order to successfully transition into the rest of their adult lives.

Crossroads has also become involved locally by establishing relationships with Cincinnati-based organizations involved in the fight for justice and engaging volunteers to participate in meaningful projects. Crossroads helped found the Cincinnati Rescue and Restore Coalition, a group that both raises awareness regarding human trafficking and seeks to mobilize local services for victims. Further, in cooperation with the National Underground Railroad Freedom Center's Partnership for Human Freedom and Polaris Project, Crossroads volunteers (attorneys, researchers, and social workers) have written a comprehensive report on human trafficking in Cincinnati.

121 Community Church—Grapevine, TX

Planted in 1999, 121CC[2] is still quite a young church. Their journey toward justice ministry began a few years ago as part of the church's five-year anniversary celebration. The leadership wanted to incorporate something special into the festivities that would focus some of the celebration energy in an outward, missional direction. They took on five huge home makeover projects in the community as a way to celebrate. Issues of compassion have always been part of the DNA at 121, and completing these projects was a joy for all involved.

A few years later, having just finished a long expository series on Romans, senior pastor Ross Sawyers began a sermon series everyone remembers: a study of the book of Amos. At the hands of the prophet Amos, 121 entered a challenging Encounter phase. To everyone's surprise, church attendance increased during this period, even during the summer months. The congregation was struck by the pervasiveness of justice in the Bible's books of prophecy and the realization that much of God's anger with Israel related to their lack of justice. These realizations led to several questions—not only, "What is the church going to do?" but the more personal, "What am *I* going to do?"

At the same time, 121 was embarking on a capital campaign for a facility expansion. They decided to add about 30 percent to the overall campaign and use the resulting $300,000 to develop some new justice ministry based on all they had been learning. The success of the campaign led to a whole new challenge—how and where and for what they would use these new funds. This became the job of Rodney Howell, mission/equipping pastor. The availability of this significant funding kicked off 121's Explore phase and gave it a sense of urgency. The church formed four different teams—for research, prayer, communication, and engagement—and tasked them to discern what God already had prepared for them to do (see Ephesians 2:10).

It is fascinating to note that up to this point, staff and congregants at 121 had never heard of IJM. But clearly the path they were following was a version of the Encounter, Explore, Engage process outlined in this book. It would be their Explore work that would lead 121 to IJM. The four teams that the church had formed worked roughly simultaneously. A justice devotional was created that the entire congregation was encouraged to use. Meanwhile, the research team narrowed down their area of focus to children at risk. The church researched connections with orphanages and eventually arrived at a connection with IJM via one of our aftercare partners in Cambodia.

Soon after initial contact was made, an IJM church mobilization director came to 121 and met with key leaders in the justice effort. As trust grew, IJM became interested in seeing 121 involved in the work in Cambodia. Discerning that 121 had the capacity to support aftercare work, the church mobilization director eventually set up a trip for 121's research team leaders to travel to Cambodia and meet the aftercare partners there.

While there, the team from 121 also led a spiritual retreat for the IJM team. The retreat was a great encouragement to IJM Cambodia. Over the course of about a year, in connection with IJM, 121 decided to make a deep investment in IJM and aftercare in Cambodia. They began supporting IJM's work in Cambodia with a significant contribution from the justice fund.

One member of the congregation, Alf, attended the Global Prayer Gathering. Deeply impacted by the experience and all that he was learning at 121, Alf and his wife, Kelly, began serious discussions about moving to Cambodia. At the time of this writing, Alf and Kelly are in an intentional preparation process and will soon be the physical representatives of 121's justice ministry on the ground in Cambodia—specifically in Siem Reap, a town in the north where IJM has presence alongside aftercare partners. Alf and Kelly became aware that a large highway (the Trans Asian Highway) is being built across Laos, Vietnam, Thailand, and Cambodia. It will go right through Siem Reap, and this new transit corridor will likely increase human trafficking. Representatives from 121 would like to be there to lend a hand.

Most recently, 121 hosted an event to raise awareness of justice issues while raising funds for the work in Cambodia. The organizers created an event called Run4Justice. Not actually runners themselves, the organizers set a goal to recruit 1,000 participants and raise $100,000. When people heard about their ambitious goals, some of them (actual runners) tried to prepare the organizers by suggesting that 250 runners would be a more realistic goal, especially for a first-year event. In the end, the event was a huge success, with over 1,300 runners participating and raising over $140,000! The organizers created a huge wall for the day of the event. The eight-foot-tall structure stretched roughly forty feet. Each panel of the wall depicted a step in the process of human trafficking and rescue in Cambodia. It was an emotionally moving educational tool.

Recently I asked our friends at 121 how often the issue of biblical justice comes up in their Sunday services these days. I thought their response was both interesting and healthy. They said that because Ross, their senior pastor, is an expository preacher and the issue of justice is all over the Bible, it can come up at almost any time. And these days, with all of the different people at 121 who are engaged in the work of justice, it comes up much more frequently than it used to.

Kingdom of God Church—Airoli, Navi Mumbai, India

When he attended a conference hosted by IJM Mumbai, Pastor Guy had a deep encounter with the issue of human trafficking and its impact on the vulnerable girls and women in his city. Deeply moved by the suffering of the victims as well as the nature of the response IJM was organizing, Pastor Guy says, "God put it on my heart to help."

Living in the same vicinity as an IJM field office opens some interesting possibilities for congregations like Kingdom of God Church to offer direct support to the work. But this support often comes in the form of risks that pull members and pastors alike far out of their comfort zones. One such opportunity arises in the form of the need for independent witnesses. Under Indian law, the testimony of police officers alone does not carry the necessary weight to convict perpetrators of commercial sexual exploitation. As a result, IJM cases are greatly strengthened by the presence of two independent witnesses—one man and one woman. The role of an independent witness is not simple or easy. Careful observation of the operation conducted by the local authorities takes the better part of a day. Over the course of their observations, the witnesses are exposed to the bleak suffering trafficking visits upon its victims. Witnesses are then asked to assist with the documentation of the operation, painstakingly recalling every possible fact. When the case reaches trial, often as many as three years later, witnesses are required to testify confirming their original statement and to undergo cross-examination. This process can extend over several court dates requiring lengthy travel to and from the courthouse each time.

When Pastor Guy invited his congregation to step forward and volunteer as independent witnesses, one brave soul responded: a woman named Rekha. Because Rekha's husband was uneasy about letting her take this risk, Pastor Guy volunteered to go with her. Soon both were called to serve their independent witness function in an IJM-assisted operation. The night of the operation was difficult. Pastor Guy describes the inside of the brothel as "stinking." As they witnessed the operation unfold, and particularly as Pastor Guy saw the existence these girls had been subjected to, he says, "I felt totally broken." He and Rekha stayed at the police station until late in the night helping to process documentation on the eight young women who had been rescued.

In the days following the operation, Pastor Guy was thoughtful about the experience and about the new life these girls were living. The next evening he shared with his wife that "these girls had lived one whole day without their bodies being touched or ravaged. What an experience, . . . being in that kind of slavery and then one day later, they were actually able to experience freedom."

Seven months later, Rekha was called by the public prosecutor to testify in the case against the alleged perpetrators who had been arrested during the operation she had observed. Already caring for three small children at home, she had just entered her ninth month of pregnancy. Rekha's husband took time off work to accompany her to the court for her testimony (a huge sacrifice for an auto rickshaw driver). She told the story of what she had seen that night seven months earlier. As her testimony ended, Rekha was asked to return the next day for cross-examination by the defense. In spite of the cost and her advanced pregnancy, she willingly returned and answered every question posed by the defense.

As of the writing of this book, this case is still in process in the Indian court. We continue to pray that justice will be done on behalf of these eight victims.

As for Pastor Guy, having seen the reality of commercial sexual exploitation and taken the risk to engage, he says flatly, "My life will never be the same." Though he sees his own role in this one operation as a small one—allowing the police to "use my eyes to see"—Pastor Guy is encouraged. He's become a tireless advocate wanting to encourage people that "we *can* do something."

Discovery Church—Orlando, FL

In 2007, Discovery Church invited an IJM speaker to share the message of biblical justice during the weekend services. This began an ongoing connection between IJM and Discovery that continued to grow.

In 2009 Discovery invited IJM back to preach again. As I prepared to share with the congregation, IJM's field office director in one of our India offices approached me and laid out the aftercare challenge his team was facing. There were two basic issues. First, the state-run homes that did exist were woefully understaffed and underfunded, rendering them simply incapable of providing a minimum standard of quality care. While the few staff the homes did have were dedicated and caring, there simply were not enough resources. Second, it surprised the field office director that given the global Christian community's outrage about issues of trafficking, there was no one at all following God's call to care for victims by actually creating aftercare homes in his city. This field office director was wondering aloud if there might be some church in the IJM family—some courageous church—that would be willing to take the huge risk of opening a brand-new aftercare home. I immediately thought of Discovery. I called them the same day and presented the opportunity.

As we talked about the possibility, there was a familiar mixture of fear and faith—a sense that God just might be in the midst of it all, inviting Discovery to take a risk. Discovery said yes. We scrambled to iron out the details in time for the engagement. There was an Indian organization eager to partner with Discovery. They even had a building they could donate to be remodeled into the aftercare home itself. What was desperately needed were the funds to run the home. It would cost on the order of $50,000 per year for start-up and staffing costs. As the weekend services at Discovery approached, pastor David Loveless decided that the best way forward would be to present the need to the congregation and invite them to be generous. They weren't sure they could raise the $50,000 needed for the first year of operations, especially as the congregation and the church staff had been hit hard by recession. But as David said several times through the process, "This just feels like something God is doing."

During each of the weekend services, an IJM church mobilization staffer preached a message on biblical justice (in this case, I had the privilege of being one of them). Then David Loveless explained the opportunity that lay before Discovery. He made reference to the difficult economic times the church had been through but said clearly and passionately that "this just seems like something God is doing." The people of Discovery seemed to agree. By the end of the weekend, they had generously contributed enough funds to operate the new aftercare home for three years! The gifts—totaling over $150,000—had included two Rolex watches that a couple decided to contribute.

There were many details to work out. A team from Discovery traveled to India to meet the partner organization, an indigenous Christian ministry with decades of experience. The group toured many of the state-run aftercare homes and spent time with IJM's aftercare staff. There was a lot of conversation about the nature of this three-way partnership, ending in the drafting of a careful memorandum of understanding that would guide the development and operation of the new home.

The building was remodeled into a beautiful aftercare facility. And in March 2010, an operating license was granted by the Indian government. The completion and licensing of the home coincided with a large IJM-led operation on a brothel that freed dozens of young women. So on the day the home opened, it was filled to capacity (twenty-three clients). This home is far and away the highest-quality aftercare facility we know of nationwide. Discovery's generosity allowed for it to be constructed and staffed according to IJM's carefully developed best practices. It is the place where survivors of trafficking are offered new life, life more abundant than they had dared to hope for.

Being involved with IJM has also helped Discovery to consider what they might be able to do locally in Orlando. Being there to see big things happen in India has given them an appetite for some big projects at home. Based on what they've learned overseas, they've decided to carefully focus their local efforts. Instead of broad involvement with the city, they are focusing on one neighborhood and going deep to provide services in the areas of sanitation, security, and safety.

Kimber Liu is the director of Discovery's LoveWorks, the missional arm that oversees the church's involvement both locally and in India. Recently I asked her what involvement in this justice ministry has changed about her as a disciple of Jesus. She thought for a minute and said, "Most of my life—even as a leader and a pastor—has been involved in the parts of Scripture that deal with *me*. Now I'm also focused on the parts of Scripture that deal with loving my neighbor."

Kolkata Christian Fellowship—Kolkata, India

When IJM first established a field office in Kolkata, several staff members began to attend worship and become involved in

Kolkata Christian Fellowship (KCF). According to KCF's pastor, Ashok Andrews, this "radically changed the life and course of the church." Through its connection to IJM, the church became much more aware of issues of violence and oppression in its own community. They also had an encounter with what Pastor Ashok calls "the Father's heart of justice." KCF began to involve itself in small ways with what the IJM team was doing. They engaged in prayer, provided independent witnesses wherever possible, encouraged the IJM staff, and celebrated each new victory as operations accomplished the deliverance of young girls from the hell of trafficking. What they found as they engaged, Pastor Ashok reports, is that this involvement led to the transformation of the church's own members. The KCF family was so impacted that they talked about God's heart for justice wherever they went. This impact was felt in a sister organization of Kolkata Christian Fellowship called JKPS, an organization with decades of ministry experience among the poor in India. Because Pastor Ashok also serves as the leader of JKPS, this passion for justice spread very naturally through both organizations.

Gradually, the Christian community in Kolkata became more and more aware of the absence of Christian aftercare in the city. As IJM spoke of this dire need, the families of KCF and JKPS prayed, asking God to move and for those in the Christian community to work at a solution to this significant problem. But because they felt inadequate and ill equipped for the task, neither KCF nor JKPS imagined involving themselves directly in the solution.

But then, in Pastor Ashok's words, "a series of miracles" happened. Partners International, Canada (JKPS's single biggest partner over the years), purchased a building, intending that JKPS use it to "care for the marginalized and hurting." As JKPS prayed over the specific use of the building, God burdened them with the need for aftercare. Their response was humble and courageous: "If God wants us to stand in the gap, we will!" JKPS and Partners International, Canada, agreed to renovate the building for use as an aftercare home. IJM provided technical expertise regarding programming and standards of care in the home. God moved in clearly miraculous ways to provide a license to run this new aftercare program in record time. And finally, as you may have already guessed, Discovery Church in Orlando rounded out the partnership, agreeing to provide funding for all of the staff the home would require. What Pastor Ashok loves about this partnership is that it is a picture of "the body of Christ from all over the world joining hands and forces in order that young girls can be given dignity, care, love, and hope."

To this day, Discovery Church continues to provide resources for the staffing of the home. Partners International, Canada, has continued to meet the ongoing running expenses. IJM has been a catalyst and a champion in assisting with all technical matters concerning the home. Pastor Ashok says, "The JKPS family rejoices that God has counted them worthy of this incredible task, and the family of KCF continues to rejoice that they are able to provide as much spiritual support to the home as possible."

Today, this home is considered an exceptional aftercare home in Kolkata.

New Heart Community Church—La Mirada, CA

In chapter 6 I told the story of Mae, a marriage and family therapist from The River. She chose to embrace risk by becoming the director of aftercare in a brand-new IJM field office in the Philippines. I mentioned in that chapter that Mae and her team have done a fantastic job of bringing justice in cases of commercial sexual exploitation of minors. But as you can imagine, there have been some challenges along the way. Mae's job can be fairly stressful.

Because of this, once a year, Mae steps out of this role for about a month. She returns to the United States to recuperate and rest and to visit with her family, many of whom also live there. Mae's first furlough was particularly welcome. Aside from missing her family, the adjustments of the first year in the Cebu office had taken their toll. The start of any new IJM office is a challenge, and Cebu was no exception. With respect to aftercare in particular, Mae left the Philippines with a weighty concern on her shoulders. IJM was having trouble finding appropriate aftercare for survivors of commercial sexual exploitation. The lack of quality aftercare was becoming a limiting factor in the advance of IJM's work in Cebu. Without more aftercare capacity, it would be difficult to continue working with local law enforcement to rescue more victims of sex trafficking—they would have nowhere to go.

In the midst of this concern, Mae was cautiously optimistic about some recent communication she'd had with a church in Southern California called New Heart. Staff at New Heart had contacted IJM in Washington, DC, after reading *Good News about Injustice*. During a process much like the Encounter and Explore phases outlined in this book, New Heart had discovered a passion for biblical justice, fairly extensive connections in the Philippines, and a deep desire to engage—particularly in aftercare. Because of these interests, my church mobilization colleagues forwarded New Heart's e-mail to Mae in the Philippines. What made this e-mail stand out to her was the name of the New Heart pastor who had written it. Mae recognized him as the adviser to the Filipino student's association she'd been involved with years before as an undergrad at Biola.

New Heart invited Mae to speak during her upcoming furlough.

Mae shared a message of biblical justice with the congregation. She spoke from her own experience of working with survivors of commercial sexual exploitation in Cebu. Mae's presence and message confirmed what God had already been doing among leaders and congregants at New Heart. New Heart had been in the midst of a building campaign and looking forward to moving out of the school they were renting and into a more permanent facility. But their encounter with the God of justice had triggered a whole new idea.

They had come to the realization that New Heart didn't need a building nearly as much as trafficking survivors in Cebu needed a viable aftercare facility. They shut down their capital campaign and agreed to invest the money in starting an international nonprofit organization that would start and run a brand-new aftercare facility.

It is not uncommon for a church to *want* to do this. What is positively rare are churches willing to take risks involved in actually trying to do it. Within months, New Heart had set up a US–based 501(c)(3) organization that could serve as a funding conduit for this new initiative. With dizzying speed, they hired an experienced Filipino national as the in-country director who began the search for a building and for qualified staff to run the facility. They met with many challenges. They prayed. They risked. It was hard. But the astonishing fact is that today there stands in Cebu a brand-new aftercare facility called My Refuge House that is serving girls and women IJM has rescued from commercial sexual exploitation. This home has been built by the risky generosity of New Heart church.

The scope of this project likely makes it seem out of the reach of many churches. As I have told this story many times over the last few years, the reaction I often get is, "Oh, that's great! Those large Southern California churches have so much capacity for complex projects." I take some pleasure in the shock on people's faces when I tell them that New Heart is a church of eighty-five people!

Cornerstone Fellowship—Livermore, CA

As a young church, Cornerstone has always been missional in the sense that leaders and members of the church are not content to live with a disconnect between what they *know* and what they *do*. Also as a young church, they are eager to develop meaningful ministry at home and constructive ministry relationships around the world. So when Cornerstone invited IJM to speak at their weekend services in 2008, people were ready. In the words of Chris Stockhaus, Cornerstone's serve pastor, "There was an amazing response to the message." The whole church became excited about the idea of engaging the issue of justice and doing it in partnership with IJM.

Following the weekend services, at least thirty people came forward indicating that they would like to be part of a Justice Learning Community, many of whom had already made the individual decision to become IJM Freedom Partners. The group helped the entire church experience an encounter with injustice and the God of justice, and soon transitioned into task-force mode. They contacted local organizations, heard presentations, and began to evaluate what Cornerstone should do. This Justice Task Force phase took most of a year, and during this time, several Cornerstone members became IJM Justice Advocates.

Several Cornerstone members attended the Global Prayer Gathering in 2009. In one of the prayer rooms, they were asked to pray for the economic self-sufficiency and reintegration of the children IJM had rescued from the commercial sex industry in the Philippines. This need struck a chord for them.

Later that year, one of IJM's field office directors contacted me regarding this same need. The field office was wondering if I might be able to find a church that could help them with a reintegration project they had been incubating for about six months. I immediately thought of Cornerstone.

In the summer of 2009, I met with the senior staff at Cornerstone and presented about two hundred pages of research conducted by IJM's team in the Philippines. The research included a thorough study of the current aftercare systems in place, the gaps that existed, and what would be required for successful reintegration of trafficking survivors. In the end, the study proposed a solution with the working title "Economic Self-Sufficiency and Reintegration Project" (ESSR). I explained that this project was desperately needed. And while the IJM team was currently developing the program on a small scale, it was clear our team did not have the resources to continue, much less to scale it up. I asked Cornerstone if they would consider taking on this project as their own—essentially becoming an IJM aftercare partner in the field. Though the level of complexity and the cost were both high, Cornerstone was excited to explore the possibility further.

The following January, I found myself in the Philippines with a small team from Cornerstone. Over the course of ten days, the team met several aftercare partners and learned about the work firsthand. Then we began serious conversation about what it would look like for Cornerstone to take on this project. There were many complex questions to unravel.

The Cornerstone team returned home and worked to discern if this was a project for them. Chris was the first one to buy in and say he felt God was calling them to engage. And engage they did. Chris and his team worked out a clear plan. The church set up an international NGO that could operate in the Philippines.

They raised money and began hiring staff—most of whom are Filipino. Astonishingly it took Cornerstone less than a year from their initial trip to the Philippines to begin operating a functional NGO called the Red Window Project.

There is no doubt that the project has been a lot of hard work. But the fact is that the Red Window Project is one of only a few organizations we know of in the world working at trafficking-survivor reintegration in a concrete and measurable way. And by God's grace, they are experiencing success. I found Chris's perspective on all this quite refreshing. When I asked him what he liked most about being involved in Red Window, he said, "This is the type of project where your faith grows so much—because you see God working from day one." He said that one of the most amazing moments of the reintegration process is the shift that happens in the clients' lives when they realize that they *do* have viable options other than the abuse they've come from. As part of their training, they tour a hotel or a call center and see what it's like to work there. They all are captivated and immediately want to begin working at these places.

Local churches in Cebu have engaged with Red Window as well. Several churches, for example, have begun tutoring IJM and Red Window clients in English.

The Final Word

THE ADVENT OF THE MODERN GPS has changed my life. Despite my terrible sense of direction, I can now find my way to any location on planet earth, provided I know its address or coordinates. With my destination entered into the system, I can start my journey confidently. I don't have to have even the vaguest idea of where I'm going. I don't even need to know if my destination is north or south of my current position. I just plug in the address and off I go.

It may be tempting to see the specific information, especially in the later chapters of this book, as a kind of GPS to guide you to the work of justice ministry. Unfortunately, not only would that be an oversimplification, it would yield underwhelming results. A GPS is a fantastic tool to get you to a specific, known destination. But it's not the best system for exploring new territory.

The journey this book describes is much more like an expedition somewhere new and unknown. It's much more like orienteering—like trekking in the wilderness. The orienteer takes a small set of trusted tools (usually a compass and a topographical map) and skillfully uses them to navigate a course through unfamiliar territory. The tools I have described in this book are much more like a compass and a map than they are like a turn-by-turn GPS. A skilled orienteer can use these simple tools to explore without needing to have a fixed destination in mind. In fact, I want to encourage you to begin this journey *without* an end point in mind—without a fixed idea of what sort of justice ministry destination you might arrive at. Doing so will leave you open to discover unknown destinations even greater than those you might be tempted to set out for—higher peaks, seemingly endless plains, exhilarating river rapids. This process is an invitation to explore the uncharted territory of justice ministry and to discover deepening faith, purpose, and joy along the way.

These tools may be new to you, and the landscape may be more challenging than you are used to, but the wonderful promise of God is that you do not head off into this wilderness alone. In fact, you are called to this journey by a God who loves and cares for you. You are invited on this adventure by a God who is in the habit of using the pilgrimage to transform the pilgrim. And while your love for God and for the vulnerable you seek to serve will be good fuel for the journey, it will be vital to remember that you know these loves only in shadow form—and that you know them only because God first loved you. So take courage and take humility. Gather your friends and be on your way.

Acknowledgments

EXACTLY HOW a pile of hard work becomes an intelligible book is a mystery that has been solved for me by a community of people who deserve more thanks than I have the talent to offer with mere words. I am deeply thankful to those who helped shape and focus my early thinking, including Kimberly Pendleton Bolles. There were many early readers of the manuscript who offered invaluable encouragement and feedback. Among them are Larry Martin, Bethany Hoang, Chong-Ae Shah, Kathryn Witzke, and my daughter Charlotte. I'm also thankful for my colleagues on the IJM Church Mobilization team (past and present) whose faithful work with churches produced much of what became the second half of this book (and without whom my job would be a lot less fun): Christa Hayden, Mike Hogan, Andy Hein, Lauren Johnson, Brittany Cress, and Mark Kirchgestner. I am, by now, forever indebted to the deeply talented Lori Foley Poer, whose wisdom and skill as IJM's senior editorial manager far exceed her years. And the tireless work of my IJM colleague Amy Lucia ensured that this manuscript was seriously considered by just about every publisher of English-language books. Thanks also to Jan Long Harris for championing this project with Tyndale and to Jonathan Schindler for his careful editing.

I am inspired by the partnership of many wonderful friends who have embraced faithful risk as a pathway to deep discipleship. Among them, of course, are my colleagues in IJM's field and partner offices. I'm also profoundly grateful for those who have, by their own faithfulness, been God's instruments to form and shape me. Among them are many great friends at The River Church Community and especially Brad Wong, without whom my time at The River would have been only half as sweet.

Finally, if grace can be defined as unmerited favor, then among God's great expressions of grace to me is my wife, Jenna, whom I simply do not deserve. She and our children Clara, Charlotte, and Aidan continue to be the main characters in the life stories that give me deep and lasting joy.

100% of author royalties will further the work
of International Justice Mission.

Justice Materials for Further Study

Further Study on Justice from a Biblical Perspective

Bonhoeffer, Dietrich. *Ethics*. New York: Simon & Schuster, 1995.

———. *Letters and Papers from Prison*. New York: Simon & Schuster, 1997.

Crouch, Andy. *Culture Making: Recovering Our Creative Calling*. Downers Grove, IL: InterVarsity, 2008.

Haugen, Gary. *Good News about Injustice: A Witness of Courage in a Hurting World*. Downers Grove, IL: InterVarsity, 1999.

———. *Just Courage: God's Great Expedition for the Restless Christian*. Downers Grove, IL: InterVarsity, 2008.

Keller, Timothy. *Generous Justice: How God's Grace Makes Us Just*. New York, NY: Dutton Adult, 2010.

Labberton, Mark. *The Dangerous Act of Loving Your Neighbor: Seeing Others through the Eyes of Jesus*. Downers Grove, IL: InterVarsity, 2010.

———. *The Dangerous Act of Worship: Living God's Call to Justice*. Downers Grove, IL: InterVarsity, 2007.

Lewis, C. S. *God in the Dock*. Grand Rapids, MI: Eerdmans, 1994.

Perkins, John. *Let Justice Roll Down*. Ventura, CA: Regal Books, 2006.

Sherman, Amy. *Kingdom Calling: Vocational Stewardship for the Common Good*. Downers Grove, IL: InterVarsity, 2011.

Stearns, Richard. *The Hole in Our Gospel: What Does God Expect of Us?* Nashville, TN: Thomas Nelson, 2009.

Wright, Christopher J. H., *The Mission of God: Unlocking the Bible's Grand Narrative*. Downers Grove, IL: InterVarsity, 2006.

General Human Rights Reading

Bales, Kevin. *Disposable People: New Slavery in the Global Economy.* Berkeley: University of California Press, 2004.

Dallaire, Roméo. *Shake Hands with the Devil: The Failure of Humanity in Rwanda.* New York: Da Capo Press, 2004.

Hochschild, Adam. *Bury the Chains: Prophets and Rebels in the Fight to Free an Empire's Slaves.* New York: Houghton Mifflin, 2005.

————. *King Leopold's Ghost: A Story of Greed, Terror, and Heroism in Colonial Africa.* New York: Mariner Books, 1999.

Human Rights Watch. *Human Rights Watch World Report.* Published annually. http://www.hrw.org.

Kara, Siddharth. *Sex Trafficking: Inside the Business of Modern Slavery.* New York: Columbia University Press, 2009.

Kidder, Tracy. *Mountains Beyond Mountains: The Quest of Dr. Paul Farmer, a Man Who Would Cure the World.* New York: Random House, 2004.

Kristof, Nicholas D., and Sheryl WuDunn. *Half the Sky: Turning Oppression into Opportunity for Women Worldwide.* New York: Knopf, 2009.

Paton, Alan. *Cry, the Beloved Country.* New York: Simon & Schuster, 2003.

Power, Samantha. *"A Problem from Hell": America and the Age of Genocide.* New York: Harper Perennial, 2007.

US Department of State. *The Trafficking in Persons Report.* Published annually. http://www.state.gov/j/tip/rls/tiprpt.

Wiesel, Elie. *Night.* New York: Farrar, Straus and Giroux, 2006.

Videos

Video is an extraordinarily powerful tool for storytelling and education. In order to resource churches with current and effective tools, IJM is constantly producing new video materials of many different types. From thirty-minute documentaries on the nature of violent oppression in the world to shorter client interviews, we have a variety of videos suitable for discussion in small groups or among friends. We also have very short pieces suitable for the weekend service setting, and we are producing more all the time. For a current list of available videos, visit www.ijm.org. You may also visit IJM's Vimeo site at http://vimeo.com/ijm.

Web Resources for Further Research on International Justice Issues

There are many groups working on international justice issues; this is not an attempt to list them. Rather, the websites below each have considerable research resources—from statistics to country reports—that may be useful during and beyond your Encounter phase.

International Justice Mission: www.ijm.org
Amnesty International: www.amnesty.org
Freedom House: www.freedomhouse.org
Human Rights Watch: www.hrw.org
International Criminal Court: www.icc-cpi.int
International Labour Organization: www.ilo.org
UNICEF (United Nations Children's Fund): www.unicef.org
University of Minnesota Human Rights Library:
    www.umn.edu/humanrts
UN Office of the High Commissioner for Human Rights:
    www.ohchr.org
US Department of State Bureau of Democracy, Human Rights, and Labor: www.state.gov/g/drl
US Department of State Office to Monitor and Combat Trafficking in Persons: www.state.gov/g/tip

Understanding Justice Issues at Home
Polaris Project

Polaris Project is a leading organization in the United States combating all forms of human trafficking and serving both US citizens and foreign national victims, including men, women, and children. http://www.polarisproject.org

Slavery Footprint

The Slavery Footprint website allows consumers to visualize how their consumption habits are connected to modern-day slavery. Through their Free World mobile app and online action center, Slavery Footprint provides consumers an outlet to voice their demand for things made without slave labor. http://slaveryfootprint.org

US Government Resources
The Campaign to Rescue and Restore Victims of Human Trafficking

This division of the US Department of Health and Human Services offers help in identifying victims, raising awareness, and assisting victims of human trafficking. www.acf.hhs.gov/trafficking

Office to Monitor and Combat Trafficking in Persons

A division of the US Department of State, this organization partners with foreign governments and civil society to confront modern slavery. www.state.gov/g/tip

Justice-Related Scriptures

The LORD your God is God of gods and Lord of lords, the great God, mighty and awesome, who is not partial and takes no bribe, who executes justice for the orphan and the widow, and who loves the strangers, providing them with food and clothing. (Deuteronomy 10:17-18)

He will judge the world in righteousness; he will govern the peoples with justice. (Psalm 9:8, NIV)

The LORD is known by his acts of justice; the wicked are ensnared by the work of their hands. (Psalm 9:16, NIV)

O LORD, you will hear the desire of the meek; you will strengthen their heart, you will incline your ear to do justice for the orphan and the oppressed, so that those from earth may strike terror no more. (Psalm 10:17-18)

For the LORD is righteous, he loves justice; the upright will see his face. (Psalm 11:7, NIV)

He loves righteousness and justice; the earth is full of the steadfast love of the LORD. (Psalm 33:5)

Your righteousness is like the highest mountains, your justice like the great deep. You, LORD, preserve both people and animals. (Psalm 36:6, NIV)

He will make your vindication shine like the light, and the justice of your cause like the noonday. (Psalm 37:6)

Your throne, O God, will last for ever and ever; a scepter of justice will be the scepter of your kingdom. (Psalm 45:6, NIV)

No, in your heart you devise injustice, and your hands mete out violence on the earth. (Psalm 58:2, NIV)

They plot injustice and say, "We have devised a perfect plan!" Surely the human mind and heart are cunning. (Psalm 64:6, NIV)

I will sing of loyalty and of justice; to you, O LORD, I will sing. (Psalm 101:1)

The LORD works vindication and justice for all who are oppressed. (Psalm 103:6)

Happy are those who observe justice, who do righteousness at all times. (Psalm 106:3)

It is well with those who deal generously and lend, who conduct their affairs with justice. (Psalm 112:5)

I know that the LORD maintains the cause of the needy, and executes justice for the poor. (Psalm 140:12)

It is not good to be partial to the wicked and so deprive the innocent of justice. (Proverbs 18:5, NIV)

When justice is done, it is a joy to the righteous, but dismay to evil-doers. (Proverbs 21:15)

The righteous care about justice for the poor, but the wicked have no such concern. (Proverbs 29:7, NIV)

Learn to do good; seek justice, rescue the oppressed, defend the orphan, plead for the widow. (Isaiah 1:17)

His authority shall grow continually, and there shall be endless peace for the throne of David and his kingdom. He will establish and uphold it with justice and with righteousness from this time onward and forever-more. The zeal of the LORD of hosts will do this. (Isaiah 9:7)

Therefore the LORD waits to be gracious to you; therefore he will rise up to show mercy to you. For the LORD is a God of justice; blessed are all those who wait for him. (Isaiah 30:18)

Here is my servant, whom I uphold, my chosen, in whom my soul delights; I have put my spirit upon him; he will bring forth justice to the nations. (Isaiah 42:1)

Listen to me, my people, and give heed to me, my nation; for a teaching will go out from me, and my justice for a light to the peoples. (Isaiah 51:4)

My righteousness draws near speedily, my salvation is on the way, and my arm will bring justice to the nations. The islands will look to me and wait in hope for my arm. (Isaiah 51:5, NIV)

Thus says the LORD: Maintain justice, and do what is right, for soon my salvation will come, and my deliverance be revealed. (Isaiah 56:1)

Is not this the fast that I choose: to loose the bonds of injustice, to undo the thongs of the yoke, to let the oppressed go free, and to break every yoke? (Isaiah 58:6)

Truth is lacking, and whoever turns from evil is despoiled. The LORD saw it, and it displeased him that there was no justice. (Isaiah 59:15)

For I the LORD love justice, I hate robbery and wrongdoing; I will faithfully give them their recompense, and I will make an everlasting covenant with them. (Isaiah 61:8)

O house of David! Thus says the LORD: Execute justice in the morning, and deliver from the hand of the oppressor anyone who has been robbed, or else my wrath will go forth like fire, and burn, with no one to quench it, because of your evil doings. (Jeremiah 21:12)

Woe to him who builds his house by unrighteousness, and his upper rooms by injustice; who makes his neighbors work for nothing, and does not give them their wages. (Jeremiah 22:13)

I will seek the lost, and I will bring back the strayed, and I will bind up the injured, and I will strengthen the weak, but the fat and the strong I will destroy. I will feed them with justice. (Ezekiel 34:16)

And I will take you for my wife forever; I will take you for my wife in righteousness and in justice, in steadfast love, and in mercy. (Hosea 2:19)

But as for you, return to your God, hold fast to love and justice, and wait continually for your God. (Hosea 12:6)

I hate, I despise your festivals, and I take no delight in your solemn assemblies. Even though you offer me your burnt offerings and grain offerings, I will not accept them; and the offerings of well-being of your fatted animals I will not look upon. Take away from me the noise of your songs; I will not listen to the melody of your harps. But let justice roll down like waters, and righteousness like an everflowing stream. (Amos 5:21-24)

He has told you, O mortal, what is good; and what does the LORD require of you but to do justice, and to love kindness, and to walk humbly with your God? (Micah 6:8)

And the word of the LORD came again to Zechariah: "This is what the LORD Almighty said: 'Administer true justice; show mercy and compassion to one another. Do not oppress the widow or the fatherless, the foreigner or the poor. Do not plot evil against each other.'" (Zechariah 7:8-10, NIV)

Here is my servant, whom I have chosen, my beloved, with whom my soul is well pleased. I will put my Spirit upon him, and he will proclaim justice to the Gentiles. (Matthew 12:18)

Woe to you, scribes and Pharisees, hypocrites! For you tithe mint, dill, and cummin, and have neglected the weightier matters of the law: justice and mercy and faith. It is these you ought to have practiced without neglecting the others. (Matthew 23:23)

Jesus uses the story of the "good Samaritan" serving the victim of a violent beating to illustrate what it means to be a neighbor. (Luke 10:25-37)

But woe to you Pharisees! For you tithe mint and rue and herbs of all kinds, and neglect justice and the love of God; it is these you ought to have practiced, without neglecting the others. (Luke 11:42)

This righteousness is given through faith in Jesus Christ to all who believe. There is no difference between Jew and Gentile, for all have sinned and fall short of the glory of God, and all are justified freely by his grace through the redemption that came by Christ Jesus. God presented Christ as a sacrifice of atonement, through the shedding of his blood—to be received by faith. He did this to demonstrate his righteousness, because in his forbearance he had left the sins committed beforehand unpunished—he did it to demonstrate his righteousness at the present time, so as to be just and the one who justifies those who have faith in Jesus. (Romans 3:22-26, NIV)

I saw heaven standing open and there before me was a white horse, whose rider is called Faithful and True. With justice he judges and wages war. (Revelation 19:11, NIV)

A Brief Survey of Violent Injustice in the Scriptures

These passages and stories provide some of the biblical basis for several of the types of casework IJM pursues in bringing relief to our clients around the world.

Human Trafficking

- *Joseph is sold to slave traffickers by his brothers in Genesis 37:18-36.*
- *Kidnapping to enslave or traffic is considered a capital offense in Deuteronomy 24:7.*

Illegal Detention/False Imprisonment/Abuse of Prisoners

- *Jesus is falsely accused, beaten, and killed by coercive state power in Mark 14:65ff and Luke 22:63-65ff.*
- *Paul and Silas are falsely accused, severely flogged, and jailed in Acts 16:23-24.*
- Remember those who are in prison, as though you were in prison with them; those who are being tortured, as

though you yourselves were being tortured. (Hebrews 13:3)

Slavery

- Slaves who have escaped to you from their owners shall not be given back to them. They shall reside with you, in your midst, in any place they choose in any one of your towns, wherever they please; you shall not oppress them. (Deuteronomy 23:15-16)
- Woe to him who builds his house by unrighteousness, and his upper rooms by injustice; who makes his neighbors work for nothing, and does not give them their wages. (Jeremiah 22:13; see also verses that follow)
- Now our flesh is the same as that of our kindred; our children are the same as their children; and yet we are forcing our sons and daughters to be slaves, and some of our daughters have been ravished; we are powerless, and our fields and vineyards now belong to others. (Nehemiah 5:5, where the children of the powerless are sold into slavery by the powerful)

Rape

- Alas for you who make your neighbors drink, pouring out your wrath until they are drunk, in order to gaze on their nakedness! (Habakkuk 2:15)
- *The story of Amnon's rape of Tamar is told in 2 Samuel 13:1-19. (This story is referenced on page 42 in chapter 3.)*

Illegal Land Seizure

- "Cursed be anyone who moves a neighbor's boundary marker." All the people shall say, "Amen!" (Deuteronomy 27:17)

- They have crushed and abandoned the poor, they have seized a house that they did not build. (Job 20:19)
- Do not remove an ancient landmark or encroach on the fields of orphans. (Proverbs 23:10)
- They covet fields, and seize them; houses, and take them away; they oppress householder and house, people and their inheritance. (Micah 2:2)

A Sample Encounter Strategy

I'M OFTEN ASKED by church leaders what a specific Encounter strategy might look like. While no two churches are the same and every strategy needs to be adapted to fit the local church, often a general model can serve as a helpful beginning place. What follows is an example of what a multilayered, multigenerational strategy could look like. This plan assumes you have read the material in this book and clearly understand the strategies and steps referenced in the plan.

Week Number	Activity	Notes
1	Train small-group leaders to lead six-week studies of *Good News about Injustice.*	Before offering a sermon on justice (or hosting an IJM speaker), it is essential to be ready for what will be stirred up in the hearts of the congregation. Training small-group leaders in advance will provide the opportunity for very clear and practical next steps for anyone in the congregation who feels the need to continue learning about the issue.
2 (and following)	Preach a sermon or series on biblical justice (or host an IJM speaker).	The pulpit is the most strategic place to begin. The goal should be to educate the whole congregation on the issue, offering a connection opportunity for those already passionate as well as those whose passion for justice may yet be undiscovered. (See the section "Justice in the Pulpit" on pages 122–128.)
3–8	Conduct six-week small-group studies of *Good News about Injustice.*	With the small-group leaders already trained, the church now has the capacity to involve a significant percentage of the congregation in a deeper conversation about biblical justice. The relational nature of these groups makes them perfect places to discuss the strong feelings (and sometimes personal experiences) that invariably emerge when delving into the topic of violent oppression. This can be done with existing small groups and leaders, or a set of new leaders can be vetted and trained specifically for this purpose—whatever works best for your church context.
9	Host a screening of *At the End of Slavery* (thirty-minute documentary) and discuss the formation of a Justice Learning Community (JLC).	This screening has a dual purpose. First, broadly advertised to the whole congregation, it is another excellent educational tool. Second, it is a method of gathering potential leaders for your JLC. During the previous six weeks, it will be important to stay connected with the small-group leaders in order to support them and to be kept abreast of the potential leaders who are surfacing. Develop a list of these potential JLC leaders and personally invite each one to the screening of the film. After the film, host a smaller discussion exclusively for the potential JLC leaders. Describe the role of the JLC and what the vetting process will be. Invite them into the selection process.

Week Number	Activity	Notes
10	Select a JLC.	It's important to carefully vet and select members of the JLC. Church leaders should feel very comfortable with those who will be leading the rest of the Encounter phase. Think carefully about having all who are interested actually apply and go through an interview process. It is often wise to have the opportunity to screen out some who are passionate but do not have the right skill set, or those whose personal history may make further research too traumatic for them. (Note: While a personal history of violence or sexual addiction should not exclude people from participating in the JLC, we do need to acknowledge that this material will be sensitive for some people.)
11–20	Conduct ongoing JLC research.	Appoint a lead researcher for the JLC. Task this leader with developing a research plan and interviewing all ministries of the church (expanding on the example research chart on page 134). Make sure church leadership has ongoing input into the plan as it develops.
21–24 (and following)	Execute JLC church education plan.	As the JLC develops a multifaceted plan to educate the church, appoint someone on the team to see that the plan is implemented. It will include simple things like the distribution of books to specific people in the congregation or more complex ideas like hosting a film screening for the community. It's important to understand that research and execution are two different skills. You may need to appoint different leaders to each task to ensure all of the excellent work done by the JLC is actually converted into *action*.

IJM's Community Justice Assessment Tool

IT IS CLEAR that churches who invest in the Explore process become trusted and relied-upon partners in their communities. Yet it is remarkable how few churches actually take the time to understand their surroundings well. Perhaps this is because reading and then beginning to work using the material in chapter 9 will likely lead to at least one conclusion: the task of exploring your community is quite complex. It is also true that no two communities are alike in terms of the challenges they face or the assets they represent. Therefore, the work of exploring your community requires a significant amount of discipline, wisdom, and creative energy. While the information in chapter 9 is enough to get you started, you may discover that your Justice Task Force would be better served by more specific instruction and guidance. I expect that most teams will discover just that. For this reason, IJM has produced a Community Justice Assessment Tool. This free resource is available to all churches participating in *Dive*.

Written by social worker and former IJM Cambodia aftercare director Christa Hayden, this field-tested tool is all you need to conduct a thorough assessment of your community. The sixty-page document will guide you through a six- to nine-month step-by-step process. Rather than prescribing a set approach to address injustice in every community, the tool will help you become students of your community. The nine helpful sections of the tool will guide you as you

- walk through the vital task of creating and maintaining a healthy assessment team, including guidelines for prayer, self-care, and team care;
- establish clear timelines for your assessment;
- design organizational tools for data collection;
- determine what you already know;
- identify key issues of concern;
- guide your collection of both quantitative and qualitative data;
- build expertise on specific issues of injustice and existing resources;
- develop relationships with key stakeholders;
- compile your data into an effective and compelling report; and
- design the most appropriate and effective response for your church body.

As you are likely aware from reading chapter 9, we *highly* recommend using this tool. While many churches have begun such an assessment and already function in very healthy relationships with some stakeholders in their communities, there is tremendous value in conducting a thorough, formal assessment. This tool and the knowledge your team gains as a result of using it will be the foundation on which some of the healthiest, most productive justice ministry will be built.

Notes

INTRODUCTION

1. Elizabeth Ferris, "Faith-Based and Secular Humanitarian Organizations," *International Review of the Red Cross* 87, no. 858 (June 2005), 314.
2. I find *Two-Thirds World* to be a helpful expression. For the third of us who live in the "developed" world, it can be easy to think of the Two-Thirds World as an anomaly, a minority experience that some unfortunate people in our world must contend with. I find it sobering and helpful to remember that *two-thirds* of my brothers and sisters on earth are living on two dollars per day or less and that for this majority, stable government, rule of law, and living wages are luxuries enjoyed by a privileged few living far away.
3. Christopher J. H. Wright, *The Mission of God: Unlocking the Bible's Grand Narrative* (Downers Grove, IL: InterVarsity Press, 2006), 280.
4. This is indeed important background information. For a brief survey of literature and websites offering a general overview of injustice-related suffering in today's world, see Appendix 1. There has also been wonderful work done to clearly present the justice-related content of the Scriptures. This ever-growing and extremely helpful field of scholarship is also briefly surveyed in Appendix 2.

CHAPTER 1: THE FAILURE POINT

1. IJM professionals work to provide aftercare for all clients. In each case, the aftercare program is tailored to the specific kind of abuse suffered by the client. In the case of bonded labor slavery, survivors are enrolled in a two-year program including periodic visits from a social worker, an economic development plan to equip survivors to use government-provided restitution funds toward a more secure future, and group support of other rescued slaves transitioning to a life of freedom. In South Asia, successful aftercare ensures that the vast majority of survivors will never again find themselves enslaved.

CHAPTER 2: THE NATURE OF FAITH

1. For an excellent pastoral treatment of this passage, see Spencer Perkins and Chris Rice, *More Than Equals: Racial Healing for the Sake of the Gospel* (Downers Grove, IL: InterVarsity Press, 1993), 154ff.

CHAPTER 3: FINDING TROUBLE IN THE ANDES

1. Some of this story is reprinted from my September/October 2008 *Rev!* magazine article, "Why Mercy Isn't Enough," http://www.rev.org/article .asp?ID=2993.
2. IJM and Paz y Esperanza have worked closely together in Huánuco, Peru, and Guayaquil, Ecuador, through Casework Alliance Partnerships. Recognizing their shared mission to combat the violent oppression of the poor, the two organizations have partnered specifically to address the crisis of sexual violence in these communities.
3. Throughout this book, pseudonyms have been used for the protection of victims of violent oppression.
4. For an explanation of the group's namesake, see 2 Samuel 13.

CHAPTER 4: RECOVERING FROM FAILURE

1. For an excellent, informative, and encouraging treatment of the biblical call to Sabbath and the practical outworking of Sabbath for the contemporary believer, see Marva Dawn's *Keeping the Sabbath Wholly* (Grand Rapids, MI: Eerdmans, 1989). For a simple and practical treatment of the discipline of stillness (a discipline deeply embedded in the IJM ethos), see Ruth Haley Barton's *Invitation to Solitude and Silence* (Downers Grove, IL: InterVarsity Press, 2010).
2. For more information, see Bethany Hoang, *Deepening the Soul for Justice* (Downers Grove, IL: InterVarsity Press, 2012).
3. My very great thanks to Michelle Manley, small groups pastor of The River Church Community, for introducing me to this tool, which has become invaluable to me. Michelle has steadily and patiently taught many of us at The River to rely more profoundly on the wisdom and disciplines of our spiritual ancestors. I am deeply indebted.
4. Chris Lowney, *Heroic Leadership* (Chicago: Loyola Press, 2005), 40–46.
5. Jesuits, Ignatian scholars, spiritual directors, and practitioners of the Spiritual Exercises will no doubt note that in seeking to extract the essence of the Examen for readers, I have run the risk of drastically oversimplifying it. I seek only to give credit to the spiritual genius of Ignatius as the original source of this very simple version of the Examen. For more information and a fuller treatment of the Spiritual Exercises, I recommend James L. Wakefield's *Sacred Listening* (Grand Rapids, MI: Baker Books, 2006). And for a fascinating (and quite fun) analysis of Ignatian leadership principles, I recommend *Heroic Leadership* by Chris Lowney (Chicago: Loyola Press, 2005).

CHAPTER 5: THE SECRET OF JOY

1. *tsedaqah* (tsed-aw-kaw´): rightness (abstractly), rectitude (subjectively), justice (objectively), virtue (morally), or prosperity (figuratively):—justice,

moderately, right(-eous) (act, -ly, -ness). See James Strong, *Strong's Exhaustive Concordance of the Bible* (New York: Abingdon Press, 1890), Hebrew and Chaldee Dictionary, 98. It may be interesting to note that in Spanish and French translations of the Bible, this word is most often rendered "justice." See also Mae Elise Cannon, *Social Justice Handbook: Small Steps for a Better World* (Downers Grove, IL: InterVarsity Press, 2009), 20.

CHAPTER 6: FROM MAILBOX BASEBALL TO MISSIONAL RISK

1. For more details on this landmark result achieved by Mae and her team, visit http://www.ijm.org/projectlantern.

CHAPTER 7: FINDING BETTER FUEL

1. Please note that this conversation is a composite of many I have had and not intended to represent any one interaction.
2. You may be shocked (as I was) to learn that there exists a written manual instructing people on how to become pimps. This step-by-step guide on how to acquire, subdue, control, and grow a "stable" has at times been available through mainstream online retail outlets.

CHAPTER 8: ENCOUNTER: MEETING THE GOD OF JUSTICE IN AN UNJUST WORLD

1. Physics offers us a clear (if fairly complex) explanation for this fascinating and common childhood experience. But if you've ever tried explaining it to a child, you no doubt stumbled into the same challenges (and blank stares) I did. Just tell them that as they move toward the center of the merry-go-round their *tangential* velocity decreases because their radial distance from the center is shorter. So clearly, as explained by Newton's Third Law of Motion, this causes the equal and opposite reaction of the acceleration of the merry-go-round. Then, after they've regained their equilibrium, take them out for some ice cream.
2. Judas agrees to betray Jesus in the very next paragraph of Matthew's account. And though his reasons were complex, thirty pieces of silver were offered as a payment (Matthew 26:14-15).
3. The issue of how our worldview and life experience influence our reading of the Scriptures (or any text, for that matter) is an important one. Scholars and theologians have long discussed and debated whether the reading of a text can be neutral with respect to cultural perspective. This theme is discussed at length in N. T. Wright's *The Last Word* (New York: HarperCollins, 2005), where Wright concludes, "Serious thinkers for these past few decades have long since realized that there is no such thing as a neutral perspective on anything" (p. 85).

4. This is not to suggest that poverty-related suffering and injustice-related suffering are the only kinds of suffering. Suffering is part of the human experience. My point is that churches isolated from issues of poverty and injustice tend to become consumed with the forms of suffering they experience inwardly. The lesson of the ocean sunfish (in chapter 2) is that when we open up our worldview (and our hearts) to embrace the kind of suffering experienced by billions in our world, our own, often less significant problems tend to shrink into proper perspective. And beyond that, the Scriptures can begin to come alive to us in new ways.

5. In the coming pages, I will walk you through what's involved in a detailed Encounter process. For a simplified sample Encounter strategy and timeline, see Appendix 3 on page 249. You may want to refer to that timeline as you read the specific elements of the Encounter phase. It should give you a sense of how all this fits together in the big picture. You can also visit www.ijm.org for more information on how an Encounter phase fits into IJM's church engagement program.

6. IJM has some fantastic resources in the form of sermon outlines, video clips, and actual stories of the rescue and restoration of victims and the accountability of perpetrators, which you can find at www.ijm.org.

CHAPTER 9: EXPLORE: DISCOVERING THE INTERSECTION OF TALENT, NEED, AND CALL

1. Karen Scott Collins, Cathy Schoen, Susan Joseph, et al., "Health Concerns across a Woman's Life Span: The Commonwealth Fund 1998 Survey of Women's Health," *The Commonwealth Fund,* May 5, 1999, http://www.commonwealthfund.org/Publications/Fund-Reports/1999/May/Health-Concerns-Across-a-Womans-Lifespan--The-Commonwealth-Fund-1998-Survey-of-Womens-Health.aspx.

2. A PDF of this excellent report can be found at www.childwelfare.gov/systemwide/laws_policies/statutes/clergymandated.pdf.

3. Volunteer victim advocates are trained to answer crisis hotlines and provide advocacy for many different types for victims of violence, often beginning with intake interviews at the hospital. Training and requirements vary from state to state, but a basic web search should give you all the information you need to get started.

4. More information can be found at www.strengthsfinder.com.

5. The boundary between mercy and justice ministry is defined in different ways by different people. But most churches seem to align with noted pastor and author Tim Keller's definition of mercy ministry as "the meeting of felt needs through deeds." (Timothy J. Keller, *Ministries of Mercy: The Call of the Jericho Road,* 2nd edition [Phillipsburg, NJ: P & R Publishing, 1997], 46.) As I mentioned in the introduction, over the last half century,

the church has mounted a growing response that expresses the love and light of Jesus to those suffering from all-too-common issues such as hunger, disease, and lack of clean water. But it is important to realize that there is another category of need: the need caused by violence perpetrated by the powerful against the weak. At IJM we define justice ministry as the rescue and restoration of victims of violence, the prosecution of those who abuse power, and the long-term structural transformation that ensures the poor and vulnerable are protected from victimization in the first place.

6. Contributing to these lopsided numbers is the fact that compared to the wonderful plethora of organizations doing evangelism, church planting, and mercy ministry, there are very few organizations dedicated to the work of biblical justice.

7. If you are interested in conducting a fund-raiser to support IJM's frontline work of rescue, first of all, thank you! Second, I'd encourage you to visit our website, where we have some great tools that can make this easy, including a customizable online fund-raising tool at www.ijm.org/FreedomMaker.

8. The Global Prayer Gathering brings participants very close to the reality of injustice as IJM's field office directors share concerns and challenges and invite specific prayer around very real, pressing needs. The work of intercession is interspersed with worship and surprising joy as great victories in the battle for justice are shared.

9. If you are near the Washington, DC, area or will be traveling there, you can also come and join our DC–based team for our daily time of prayer. Every IJM office around the world stops each day for prayer. In Washington, DC, we take this pause at 11:00 a.m. and often welcome visitors to join us for this time of intercession for IJM's casework and other needs. E-mail contact@ijm.org to set up a visit. You may also want to take advantage of IJM's mobile app so you can get breaking news, action items, and more.

10. If you desire a little guidance in the production of this document, I would suggest referring to the Community Justice Assessment Tool available through IJM's *Dive* program. For more information on this tool, see Appendix 4 on page 253.

CHAPTER 10: ENGAGE: MOVING FROM FEAR TO FAITH

1. There are ways that the most experienced churches participating in *Dive* can engage directly—you can learn more about these opportunities by exploring the program at www.ijm.org.

2. Gary Haugen, *Good News about Injustice* (Downers Grove, IL: InterVarsity Press, 2009), 21–22.

3. John C. Pollock, *William Wilberforce* (Belleville, MI: Lion Publishing Co., 1986), 143.

CHAPTER 11: REAL CHURCHES WITH REAL PROBLEMS

1. The volunteer work that Clay (and other professionals) pioneered with IJM has been formalized into a professional fellows program that now offers excellent opportunities for qualified professionals in many fields to directly engage in the work of justice. You can find more information on this specific program as well as more general information on IJM Zambia and the issue of illegal land seizure at www.ijm.org.

2. The name 121 Community Church is a reference to Philippians 1:21: "For to me, living is Christ and dying is gain."

International Justice Mission's global team of lawyers, investigators, and social workers are answering the Bible's call to justice by

- bringing rescue to victims of slavery, sex trafficking, and other violent oppression
- securing long-term aftercare for survivors of abuse
- pursuing accountability for perpetrators under local laws
- partnering with local authorities to transform broken public justice systems

Highlighted by *U.S. News & World Report* as one of 10 nonprofits "making a difference," IJM has been featured by the *New York Times*, *Foreign Affairs*, *Christianity Today*, National Public Radio, and CNN, among many other outlets.

Learn more at IJM.org.

CP0593

Online Discussion *guide*

TAKE *your* TYNDALE READING EXPERIENCE *to the* NEXT LEVEL

A FREE discussion guide for this book is available at bookclubhub.net, perfect for sparking conversations in your book group or for digging deeper into the text on your own.

www.bookclubhub.net

You'll also find free discussion guides for other Tyndale books, e-newsletters, e-mail devotionals, virtual book tours, and more!